# MY ANTONIA

A Play for the Stage by Charles Jones

Adapted from Willa Cather's novel
MY ANTONIA

SAMUEL FRENCH, INC.

45 West 25th Street     NEW YORK 10010
7623 Sunset Boulevard HOLLYWOOD 90046
LONDON                 TORONTO

## IMPORTANT BILLING AND CREDIT REQUIREMENTS

All producers of MY ANTONIA *must* give credit to the Adaptor of the Play in all programs distributed in connection with performances of the Play and in all instances in which the title of the Play appears for purposes of advertising, publicizing or otherwise exploiting the Play and/or a production. The name of the Adaptor *must* also appear on a separate line, on which no other name appears, immediately following the title, and *must* appear in size of type not less than fifty percent the size of the title type.

In addition the following credit must also appear in all programs and advertising used in connection with performances of the Play:

"Adapted from Willa Cather's novel
My Antonia"

**This script is dedicated to the most indomitable person in my life Eleanor Brodie Jones**

# CHARACTERS
The Antonias and the Jim Burdens

ANTONIA – (as an adult, plays ages 22 to 42)

Tony – (Antonia as a teenager, plays ages 16 to 20)

ANNIE – (Antonia as a child, age 12)

JIM BURDEN – (age 38)

JAMES – (Jim Burden as a teenager, plays ages 13 to 18)

JIMMY – (Jim Burden as a child, age 8)


## The Men
(in order of appearance)

JAKE MARPOLE – a Burden family farm hand – from Virginia

MR. SHIMERDA – Antonia's father – a musician and dreamer – from Bohemia

AMBROZ SHIMERDA – Antonia's brother – (plays ages 20-30)

MAREK SHIMERDA – Antonia's afflicted brother – Age 16 – doubles in Act II as Charley Harling, James' teenage buddy and friend

OTTO FUCHS – Burden's handyman – from Austria

KRAJIEK – A Bohemian n'er do well – doubles in Act II as Mr. Cutter – Black Hawk's lecherous moneylender

Grandfather – Josiah Burden – Jim's Grandfather – excellent farmer – tall – an Old Testament prophet

RUSSIAN PETER – heavy-set worker – doubles in Act II as Mr. Harling – father of the Harling family – a born chauvinist – successful businessman

RUSSIAN PAVEL – tall, thin – fluent in-Russian – doubles in Act II as Harry Paine a great dancer – frustrated bank clerk


The Women
(in order of appearance)


MRS. SHIMERDA – Antonia's mother – dominant and determined – from Bohemia

GRANDMOTHER – Emmaline Burden – Jim's Grandmother – a proud Virginian

MRS. HARLING – dedicated to being a perfect mother and cozy homemaker – from Ohio

FRANCES HARLING – age 24 – skilled business woman – very handsome – manages both parents well

MRS. CUTTER – a blowzy fading beauty – given to hysterics

LENA LENGARD – age 20 – beautifully dressed in clothes she has made – from Sweden

TINY SODERBALL – age 18 – perky – always wears short skirts and striped hose – from Norway

## The Children
### (in order of appearance)

LEO CUZAK – Antonia's favorite child – age 12 – blond – curly hair – looks like a little fawn

YULKA CUZAK – age 13 – dark hair – doubles in Act II as Sally Harling (the tomboy)

NINA CUZAK – age 9 – dark hair – doubles in Act II as Yulka Shimerda – Antonia's younger sister

LUCIE CUZAK – age 7 – red hair – doubles in Act II as Nina Harling (the baby)

ANTON CUZAK – age 10 – sandy hair – doubles in Act II as Harold Harling (the musician)

Note: Producers may choose to use additional couples as dancers under the pavilion and at the Fireman's Hall—if so, please note these characters as: The Marshall Field's Man; Willie O'Riley; Norwegian Mary and Bohemian Mary. In the original production Peter and Pavel did not double in speaking roles, but did appear in Act II as the Traveling Salesmen at the dances and commencement.

This adaptation was first produced by the Omaha Community Playhouse in partnership with Robert H. Ahmanson and the Ahmanson Foundation on the Playhouse Mainstage opening March 4, 1994 with the following cast in order of appearance:

Leo Cuzak ---------------------------------- Nick Gallo
Anna Cuzak --------------------------- Julie Egermayer
Yulka Cuzak---------------------------- Rachel Young
Jim Burden -------------------------- Brad Luchsinger
Antonia Cuzak ----------------------------- Julie Huff
Nina Cuzak---------------------------------- Beth Huff
Ambroz Cuzak -----------------------Andrew Thom
Lucie Cuzak --------------------------- Ashley Kelling
Anton Cuzak ----------------------- Matthew Murphy
Jimmy (Jim Burden as a child)-------Jack Waldron
Jake Marpole -----------------------Bryan McAdams
James (Jim Burden as a teenager) - Trever Pfeiffer
Mrs. Shimerda --------------------- Marianne Young
Mr. Shimerda --------------------------Keith Homan
Annie (Antonia as a child) --------------- Marie Ellis
Ambroz Shimerda ------------------------ Paul Cobb
Marek Shimerda ----------------------Andrew Thom
Yulka Shimerda ---------------------------- Beth Huff
Otto Fuchs------------------------------ Barry Wilson
Krajiek --------------------------------Alden Dunning
Tony (Antonia as a teenager)---- Christina Belford
Grandmother --------------------------Joan Hennecke
Grandfather----------------------------- John Billings
Russian Peter------------------------- Vik Dainauskas

(cont.)

Russian Pavel -------------------------- Phillip Steiner
Mr. Bushy------------------------- Donald Wieczorek
Captain Fuller ------------------------------Jack Gibbs
Mrs. Harling ------------------------Suzanne Carney
Frances Harling ----------------------Megan Lafferty
Charley Harling----------------------------Broc Bilby
Nina Harling ------------------------- Ashley Kelling
Sally Harling --------------------------- Rachel Young
Lena Lengard--------------------- Heather Hannaford
Tiny Soderball ------------------------- Kristen Perry
Mr. Harling------------------------Mike McCormack
Mrs. Cutter -------------------------- Myrna Robbins
Mr. Cutter ----------------------------Alden Dunning
Harry Paine-------------------------- Randy Stevens
Willie O'Riley----------------------- Vik Dainauskas
Norweigan Mary----------------------- Miranda Dew
Bohemian Mary----------------------Julie Egermayer
Marshall Field's Man----------------- Phillip Steiner

Onginal Production Directed by Charles Jones
Production Design by James Othuse
Assistant Director Kathryn Hammond
Stage Management by Mary Dew
Original Costume Design by Wendy Stark

The original musical score was composed by Jonathan D. Cole through a commission grant from the Omaha Playhouse Foundation. Rights for the Antonia score can be contracted through CETHECO, Inc., 803 Loveland Drive, Omaha, NE 68114. Also available is a "Foreign Language Glossary" prepared by Phillip Steiner, an invaluable tool for the use of foreign language in this script.

# Production Notes

"The little girl (Yulka) was pretty, but An$^/$-tonia—they accented it thus, strongly, when they spoke to her—was prettier."

—Willa Cather

In Nebraska, Antonia Pavleka's grandchildren and great-grandchildren, many of whom still bear the name, traditionally pronounce their name, "Ann-toe-knee-ah." The name is said quickly, with no affectation or lingering emphasis. This pronunciation is essential for realizing the poetry of Cather's lyrical phrases.

The play is set in Black Hawk, Nebraska, and nearby farms during the 1880's. The opening and closing scenes are played at the Cuzak farmyard in 1911.

The adaptation requires three players of different ages in the role of Antonia. They frequently appear onstage simultaneously, working in concert. Each should image herself as fully as possible as Antonia and never as a segment of the personality frozen at a particular point in time. Cather emphasizes repeatedly the continuing cycles of life, our adult lives are never divorced from our childhood. Nor is childhood blissfully sheltered or isolated. The role of Jim Burden is written in a parallel manner. For scripting convenience only, these roles are noted as "Antonia" – the adult, "Tony" – the teenager and "Annie" – the child. All are Antonia. The men are scripted as "Jim Burden" – the adult, "James" – the teenager and "Jimmy" – the child. All are Jim Burden. Since the trios appear as one person the players should be freely familiar, easily embracing, touching, holding one another. This could be grossly overdone, but a comfortable physical familiarity will prove helpful to the players and the audience in establishing a single persona for each trio.

Throughout the script, the cast is a team of storytellers leading and discovering the play with the audience. Narrative descriptions in the text are often intended to be spoken directly to the audience. The players should move fluidly from narrative to dialogue with no apparent adjustments in position or style.

The use of Czech, Russian, German and English are mandatory in telling Cather's *My Antonia*. At times the audience will experience a moment of isolation and disorientation similar to that of the characters. The "American Stew" was cooked across the great continental heartland as families who could not understand anything spoken by their neighbors broke the sod shoulder to shoulder. A dialogue language glossary may be obtained to facilitate the learning experience.

The primary scenic element embracing the production should be a vast stretch of sky; always changing and always the same. The small but individually detailed interior spaces should appear to be dwarfed by the sky. Designer James Othuse solved the problem of the rapid appearance of these small interiors by devising a tandem of pivoting platforms that could be dressed and re-dressed offstage then turned quickly into the performing space. His lighting lavishly enhanced the production. His use of projections provided textures, mood changes and sunflower bordered roads.

A study kit of photographs related to the homes, farms and people, used as source material by Willa Cather, is available by contacting: The Willa Cather Pioneer Memorial and Educational Foundation, Director, Patricia Phillips, 326 Webster Street, Red Cloud, Nebraska 68970. The kit includes a photocopy of the heart-stopping letter written to a young student by Antonia Pavelka, when Mrs. Pavelka was in her early eighties, detailing the family's move from Bohemia and her father's suicide. Also included is a photograph of Antonia's prized fruit cave, which still exists.

# ACT I
## Scene 1

### The Homecoming

*The Nebraska sky, a May afternoon 1911. A windmill casts LONG SHADOWS across the Cuzak farmyard as it turns. A YOUNG BOY calls excitedly to his sister as HE runs the long path up from the new roadway. SHE has been gathering apples in the orchard. Doors to a fruit cave lie upstage unnoticed.*

LEO CUZAK. (*In Czech.*) Look, look Yulka, quickly. (*In English.*) Look, look who's coming to see us!

YULKA CUZAK. Who is that? I've never seen him before! (*SHE puts down her pail of apples, to better shield her eyes from the sun.*)

LEO. Look again! It's Jim Burden! Remember? From all of Mama's stories and photographs. That's Jim Burden.

YULKA. It can't possibly be. You are wrong Leo.

LEO. Am not. Look at his clothes. That's Jim Burden.

YULKA. Probably some salesman up from Kansas City.

LEO. Not Kansas—New York City. Now run get Mama. But don't tell her who it is!

YULKA. There is nothing to tell—we don't know who . . .

LEO. (*Pushing her.*) It's Jim Burden—run—run.

YULKA. (*In Czech.*) You really are impossible, Leo.

13

*(SHE races off toward the house. LEO quickly finds a nearby hiding place. JIM BURDEN runs up from the roadway. As HE stops to catch his breath, HE speaks directly to the audience. During his narration, YULKA brings ANTONIA, dish towel in hand, running from her kitchen. The blazing afternoon sun makes it difficult for her to clearly see the visitor.)*

JIM BURDEN. I told Antonia I would come back, but life intervened and it was twenty years before I kept my promise. Nearly thirty years since our first meeting on the train. It was a shock of course. It always is, to meet people after long years, especially if they have lived as much and as hard as this woman had. The eyes that peered anxiously at me were—simply Antonia's eyes. She was there, in the full vigor of her personality, battered but not diminished.

ANTONIA. My husband's not at home, sir. Can I do anything?

JIM BURDEN. Don't you remember me, Antonia? Have I changed so much?

ANTONIA. Why, it's Jim! Yulka, it's Jim Burden! What's happened? Is anybody dead?

JIM BURDEN. No, I didn't come to a funeral this time. I got off the train at Hastings and drove down to see you and your family.

ANTONIA. *(Very excited.)* Anton, Lucie, Nina where are you all? Run Yulka, find the little boys. They're off looking for that dog, somewhere. Yulka, call Leo. Where is that Leo? You don't have to go right off, Jim? You must at least stay the night. Our older children are all off with their papa to the street fair at Wilber. Imagine, Jim, a town here in Nebraska where everyone speaks Czech! It will be such fun for them to tell us all about the fair. I won't let you go! Now that you've come you must see all the children and meet my dear, dear Anton Cuzak. You will like each other. (*The CHILDREN are racing in from all directions.*) Of course, my Martha is married now with her own baby—think of it, Jim. You saw her when she was a tiny baby herself. Maybe they can drive over, they have a Ford motorcar. (*A grand announcement, almost with tears.*) Children, this is Jim Burden.

LEO. (*Tussling his mother.*) We know who he is mother.

YULKA. Leo recognized you from all the photographs Mama has shown us and all her stories about you.

(*The Cuzak children in the play are: Leo [described by Cather as a little fawn with curly blond hair - age 12], Yulka [dark hair - age 13], Anton [sandy - age 10)] Nina [dark hair - age 9)] Lucie [red hair - age 7]. The children are barefoot, it is summer. They are well, but simply, dressed. Their skirts and trousers are short.)*

JIM. Now tell me their names and how old they are.

ANTONIA. (*Rapidly.*) This is Yulka, named for my sister, she's fifteen.

(*The CHILDREN laugh.*)

YULKA. No, Mama, I'm only thirteen.

ANTONIA. (*Pointing to Nina.*) Our Lucie is eight.

NINA. I'm Nina, Mama.

LUCIE. I'm Lucie and I'm only seven.

*(The CHILDREN are roaring with laughter.)*

ANTONIA. Anton is ten, named for his papa. This is Leo, and he's old enough to be better than he is.

LEO. *(Butting his head against his mother.)* You've forgot. You always forget mine. It's mean. Tell him, Mother.

ANTONIA. *(Ruffling his hair.)* Well, how old are you?

LEO. I'm twelve, twelve years old, and I was born on Easter Day.

ANTONIA. It's true, he was an Easter baby.

LUCIE. I was born on February 13th, so Mama says I am almost a Valentine.

ANTONIA. *(Kneeling to embrace her.)* Oh yes, Lucie is our valentine.

JIM. You are quite a family, Antonia!

LEO. We are only about half—wait till you meet the big ones. We are twelve Cuzaks in all!

ANTONIA. You wouldn't believe what it takes to feed them all! You ought to see the bread we bake on Wednesdays and Saturdays!

LUCIE. *(Lifting the apple pail to show Jim.)* We put up our own jams and jellies for our bread.

ANTONIA. Did you see all our fruit trees as you came up, Jim?

LEO. It's the best orchard in the county.

ANTONIA. *(Helping Lucie with the heavy apple pail.)* We planted every tree. I love them as if they were people. I can never feel so tired that I don't fret about those trees in a dry season. They are on my mind like the children. Many a night after their papa was asleep, I would come out and carry water to the poor things.

JIM. She had only to stand in the orchard, to put her hand on a little crab tree and look up at the apples, to make you feel the goodness of planting, tending and harvesting at last.

ANTONIA. (*Holding up the basket.*) And now we have the good of them.

YULKA. I'm afraid, Mr. Burden, Mama still works much too hard.

ANTON. But we all have our jobs and try to help out.

JIM. She has always been a hard worker. Your mother, you know, was very much loved by all of us. She was a beautiful girl.

LEO. Oh we know that!

ANTON. Everybody liked her, didn't they?

LUCIE. Your grandfather and your grandmother?

NINA. All the town people in Black Hawk!

JIM. Sometimes it doesn't occur to children that their mother was once the same age as they are now.

YULKA. She's only four years older than you, Mr. Burden.

LEO. (*Butting against Antonia again.*) And she is beauti-ful.

JIM. If you weren't nice to her, I think I'd take a club and go for the whole lot of you. You see, I know there is nobody else like her, because I was very much in love with your mother.

(*The CHILDREN giggle and seem embarrassed.*)

LEO. (*Hugging himself, then falling down.*) In love—really—in love?

ANTON. She never told us that! But she always talked lots about you and the good times you used to have.

YULKA. We've cut your picture from all the papers.

NINA. Your wife is *so* pretty.

ANTONIA. What are we thinking? Let's take Mr. Burden up to our parlor now that we have a parlor.

LEO. Can't we first show him our fruit cave?

ANTONIA. We're so proud of it, Jim, and everything keeps so nice all year long. Remember how our potatoes froze that first winter? It's a ways from the house, but there are always some of the boys who'll run out here and bring things in for me.

*(ANTON and LEO lift the cave doors.)*

NINA. Mother let us help put up the pickles and watermelon rind preserves. (*SHE exits quickly into the cave to facilitate her change as Yulka Shimerda.*)

LEO. (*Noticing his mother is crying HE embraces her with genuine concern.*) Mama, Mama, what's the matter? What's wrong?

ANTONIA. (*Hugging him.*) Nothing is wrong, my little lamb. It's just so wonderful having Mr. Burden right here with us. You have always been with me, Jim. (*Touches him.*) But now! You know, Jim, as strange as it may seem the feeling of times past are often so near I could reach out and touch them with my hand. (*SHE steps down into the cave.*)

LUCIE. Show him the spiced plums, Mother. Americans don't have those. (*SHE exits.*)

ANTON. Mother uses them to make Kolaches. (*HE exits.*)

LEO. He doesn't know about Kolaches?

*(From inside the cave ANTONIA and the CHILDREN begin singing a bright Bohemian song.)*

JIM. (*Stepping into the cave.*) You don't think I know what Kolaches are, eh? You're mistaken, young man. I've eaten your mothers Kolaches long before that Easter day you were born.

YULKA. Always too fresh, Leo. (*SHE steps into the cave.*)

*(LEO yells out his version of a wild war whoop as JIM and YULKA close the doors.)*

## ACT I
### Scene 2

### The Train

*The railway car appears DS, it is a day coach circa 1880. JIMMY is asleep across from JAKE MARPOLE. The SHIMERDA FAMILY occupies the next two seats SL. The seats are turned facing each other, and not in sequential rows.*

JAKE. (*Peeling an orange.*) Wake up, Jimmy, I done bought us some nice oranges from that newsboy and some of that candy you liked so much. Come on, Jim Burden, wake up, that there conductor said we's in Nebrasky.

JIMMY. (*To the audience.*) The most noticeable thing about Nebraska was that it was to be, Nebraska, all day long. Gimmy some of that orange, please, Jake.

JAKE. I reckon you just fell asleep a reading that book about Jesse James I bought ya'.

JAMES. (*Standing SR of the train unit, leaning on the back of Jimmy's seat.*) I remember that "Life of Jesse James" as being one of the most satisfactory books I have ever read. I was ten years old and my Virginia relatives were sending me out to my grandparents who lived in Nebraska. I had lost both my mother and father. I was in the care of a farmhand named Jake Marpole. Neither of us had ever been on a train.

*(JIMMY darts suddenly to the seat beside Jake, kneeling and peaking over the back.)*

JIMMY. Who are those folks, Jake? I didn't see them get on.

JAKE. Thems real Bohunks, Jimmy. They got on in Chicago and the conductor had to move them here while you was asleep. He apologized nicely to me for having to put foreigners right here with us. By all rights they ought to be back in the immigrant car, but it's too full and theys standing in the aisles several hours.

JIMMY. Real foreigners from across the water?

JAKE. Listen at um jabber. Cain't none of them speak good English like you and me.

ANNIE. (*Standing suddenly on her knees—nose to nose with Jimmy.*) We go Black Hawk, Nebraska. (*Pointing to herself.*) Antonia—Antonia. (*Pointing to JIMMY, who has retreated to the bottom of the seat searching for his book.*) Name?

JAKE. Well, tell her yo' name. Don't be scared, ya' cain't get no disease just talkin' to 'em.

JIMMY. Jimmy. I mean Jim, James Burden.

ANNIE. Jimmy—nice—nice name—America name.

JAKE. She has pretty brown eyes, Jimmy. I think she likes you. Yep, she likes you!

(*By now JIMMY has found his "Life of Jesse James" while pretending to be reading, HE gives Jake several quick kicks.*)

ANNIE. (*As SHE resumes her seat.*) Nice Jimmy.

(*The FAMILY speaks rapidly in Czech. [Please see Glossary for the family's dialogue.] TONY and ANTONIA have entered quickly and stand SL of the train unit, observing the scene. THEY speak to the audience over their family's conversation.*)

TONY. We danced on the cobbled roadway with our neighbors—all shouting—all weeping—all singing for joy as we set out to Prague and our journey to America. Father played his violin and the whole village danced.

ANTONIA. We were each kissed by every person in our village.

JIMMY. I had been sleeping, curled up in a red plush seat, for a long while when we reached Black Hawk. Jake roused me and took me by the hand. We stumbled down from the train to a wooden siding.

*(JAKE carries a suitcase, JIMMY his Jesse James novel. The SHIMERDAS also set off from the train. AMBROZ carries a tin trunk, MR. SHIMERDA holds his violin case in his arms. The OTHERS have personal bundles and bags. ANNIE carries a small straw suitcase.)*

JIMMY. I couldn't see any town, or even distant lights; we were surrounded by utter darkness.

*(The train pulls away leaving EVERYONE standing in inky DARKNESS—no silhouettes or shadows.)*

MRS. SHIMERDA. *(Speaking frantically in Czech.)* Is this all? No lights, no station. What is to become of us?

*(OTTO FUCHS enters USR carrying a lantern which flickers against the night. HE calls to Jake and Jimmy from DSL where HE has located their trunk—unseen until now.)*

OTTO FUCHS. Hello, are you Mr. Burden's folks? If you are, it's me you're looking for. I'm Otto Fuchs. I'm Mr. Burden's hired man, and I'm to drive you out. *(OTTO hands the lantern to JAKE and scoops JIMMY up in his arms. We can now see his big mustache and the deep scar which slices across his face.)* Hello, Jimmy, ain't you scared to come so far west?
JIMMY. Are you a desperado?

OTTO. I been a cowboy, a stage driver, a bartender, a carpenter, a miner and a farm hand but desperado ain't my line, son.

*(KRAJIEK enters US, carrying a lantern, and calls to the Shimerdas.)*

JAKE. You 'scuse Jimmy, Mr. Fuchs, he's been reading that Jesse James trash.

*(In Czech we hear KRAJIEK greeting the SHIMERDAS, who gratefully rush to him.)*

OTTO. (*Spoken over the Czech dialogue.*) Take a look, Jim, them foreign folks are going to be our nearest neighbors. They bought that pig sty that sorry Krajiek calls a farm place. I tell you he's good for nothing.

JIMMY. Where's our house?

OTTO. Only about twenty miles. We'll be there by sun up. Mr. Burden has a fine team and wagon. Your Grandfather's bought a new pony for you. I been trying him out and I'm pleased to say he's a real gentleman. His name's Dude.

*(OTTO places JIMMY on his shoulders, takes the lantern and strides offstage. JAKE runs behind carrying the suitcase and trunk. The SHIMERDAS follow Krajiek's lantern offstage. ANTONIA, ANNIE and TONY are left in the vast DARKNESS of the Nebraska night. THEY are seen in a LIMBO LIGHTING effect.)*

ANTONIA. I rode off in the back of the empty box of Mr. Krajiek's rattling old wagon.

*(The ANTONIAS sit on the floor leaning on one another.)*

ANNIE. I tried to go to sleep, but the jolting made me bite my tongue. I soon began to ache all over.

TONY. Cautiously I got up on my knees and peered over the side of the wagon. There seemed to be nothing to see, no fences, no creeks or trees.

ANNIE. No hills.

ANTONIA. Or fields.

TONY. If there was a road I could not make it out in the faint starlight.

ANTONIA. There was nothing but land, not a country at all, but the material out of which countries are made.

TONY. I had never before looked up at the sky when there was not a familiar mountain ridge against it. This was the complete dome of heaven, all there was of it.

ANNIE. I was homesick. If we never arrived anywhere, it did not matter.

ANTONIA. Between that earth and sky I felt erased, blotted out. Whatever life I might someday have I knew I must fashion it for myself.

*(THEY are enveloped by the DARKNESS and slip offstage.)*

## Act I
## Scene 3

### Jimmy's Arrival and the Garden

*Late afternoon the following day. The Burden kitchen
    pivots onstage. The room is dominated by
    Grandmother's handsome wood-burning stove, with
    warming bins above the range top. Behind the stove is a
    small dark entry to an unseen dugout storage room. To
    the left of the stove, a cupboard filled with dishes and
    cookware, DS is a serviceable kitchen table with six
    sturdy matching chairs. To the right Grandmother has
    set up a small washtub for Jimmy. As the set moves
    into place, GRANDMOTHER opens her arms to
    JIMMY, who runs in from the bedroom. HE is still
    wearing his traveling suit from the train.
    GRANDMOTHER kneels to embrace him.*

GRANDMOTHER. Had a good sleep, Jimmy?
JIMMY. Yes u'm.
GRANDMOTHER. My how you do look like your
father!
JIMMY. She had been crying, I could see. I remembered
that my father had been her little boy.
GRANDMOTHER. Here are your clean clothes they
should do just about right.

*(SHE holds them up and THEY laugh as THEY measure
    the new clothes against his body.)*

GRANDMOTHER. But first a warm bath. I have the tub ready and I'll move my old quilt rack here by the stove in case you are as shy as your father used to be.

(*JIMMY steps behind the quilt rack and begins undressing.*)

GRANDMOTHER. Now here's soap and towels.

JIMMY. I think I'm used to taking my bath without help, Grandmother. (*HE removes his clothes and begins scrubbing vigorously.*)

GRANDMOTHER. Can you do your ears, Jimmy? Are you sure?

JIMMY. Yes u'm.

GRANDMOTHER. Well now, I call you a right smart little boy.

JIMMY. What's this dark room back of the stove?

GRANDMOTHER. (*While SHE places a cloth on the table and sets out the Bible and Grandfather's spectacles.*) That's my dugout cellar. Plenty of folks nearby actually live in dugout places like that. But your Grandfather built us a real house. Now, I'm not being boastful Jimmy, but they told us when we built this place, it was the only wooden frame country house between Lincoln and the Norwegian town. Most of our neighbors have sod houses and they keep them as nice as can be, but oh my, the dirt! (*JIMMY has completed his bath and is struggling with his shoes and shirt.*) I've decided that we are not going to have supper in the dining room, but just be family together here in the kitchen. Let me help with those buttons.

JIMMY. Grandmother, I'm afraid your cakes are burning.

GRANDMOTHER. Oh no, that would never do would it? To burn up the gingerbread I made special for you. (*SHE opens the oven with heavy pot holders.*) Thank goodness Jimmy, you saved it just in time. Here try a little taste but don't burn your fingers.

JIMMY. Grandmother, how did you know gingerbread was my very favorite?

GRANDMOTHER. I somehow thought it might be. (*SHE helps him into his clean shirt.*) Just say I had every reason to believe it just might be. That must be your Grandfather stamping in from the field.

(*GRANDFATHER enters followed by JAKE and OTTO. JIM BURDEN enters and stands SL of the table, behind what will become Jimmy's chair.*
*GRANDFATHER pats Jimmy's head then THEY shake hands formally.*)

GRANDFATHER. Welcome home, son. Fuchs, Jake, ya'll washed up already? Well now, we'll stop for our prayers.

(*THEY all sit. OTTO always assists Grandmother with her chair in a courtly Austrian fashion. GRANDFATHER puts on his spectacles and places the Bible in his lap, and a hand on Jimmy's head.*)

GRANDFATHER. "He shall choose our inheritance for us, the Excellency of Jacob whom he loved. Selah."

(*THEY bow in prayer as JIM BURDEN speaks the following narration.*)

JIM BURDEN. I was awed by his intonation of the word "Selah." I had no idea what the word meant; perhaps he had not. But, as he uttered it, it became oracular, the most sacred of words.

JIMMY. (*Almost boastfully.*) Grandfather was elected a deacon in the Baptist Church after we moved to town.

*(The CAST disperses and the kitchen moves off leaving JIMMY on an open stage with the immense sky.)*

JIMMY. Early next morning I ran out of doors to explore our farmyard.

*(HE does, as GRANDMOTHER re-enters wearing a sunbonnet, carrying a grain sack and her snake cane.)*

GRANDMOTHER. Jimmy, Jimmy!

JIMMY. (*Startling her.*) Grandmother!

GRANDMOTHER. Do you want to go along with me to the garden and dig potatoes?

JIMMY. Yes u'm, I'd like to go.

GRANDMOTHER. It's near a quarter mile, mind you. Now Jimmy, this stout hickory cane with the copper tip is my rattlesnake cane. You must never go to the garden without a heavy stick or a corn knife. I've killed a great many rattlers on the way back and forth.

*(JIMMY takes the sack and holds Grandmother's hand. SHE crosses as far US as possible with JIMMY skipping beside her. THEY are quickly joined US by JAMES and JIM BURDEN. ALL FOUR turn front and*

*joyfully make the long stroll down to the audience,*
*hand in hand.)*

JAMES. I can remember exactly how the country
looked to me as I walked beside my grandmother along the
faint wagon-tracks on that early September morning. More
than anything else I felt motion in the landscape; in the
fresh, easy-blowing wind, and in the earth itself, as if the
shaggy grass were a sort of loose hide, and underneath it
herds of wild buffalo were galloping, galloping.

JIMMY. Alone, I should never have found the garden
and I felt very little interest in it when I got there. I wanted
to walk straight on through the red grass and over the edge
of the world, which could not be very far away.

*(HE and GRANDMOTHER turn back US to dig potatoes.)*

JIM. The light air about me told me that the world
ended here: only the ground and sun and sky were left, and
if one went a little farther there would be only sun and sky,
and one would float off into them.

*(ALL THREE MEN begin walking in large circles with*
*their arms outstretched, imitating the wings of great*
*birds.)*

JAMES. Like the tawny hawks which sailed over our
heads making slow shadows on the grass. I kept looking
up at the hawks that were doing what I might so easily do.

JIMMY. Grandmother, I would like to stay up here in
the garden awhile.

GRANDMOTHER. Aren't you afraid of snakes?

JIMMY. A little, but I'd like to stay anyhow.

GRANDMOTHER. (*Giving him her cane.*) Well, if you see one, don't have anything to do with him. Don't be scared if you see anything looking out of that hole in the bank over there. That's a badger hole. He's about as big as a big 'possum, and his face is striped, black and white. He takes a chicken once in a while, but I won't let the men harm him. In a new country a body feels friendly to the animals. (*With the sack of potatoes, SHE begins her exit.*)

JAMES. Grandmother swung the bag of potatoes over her shoulder and went down the path. When she came to the first bend, she waved at me and disappeared. (*The MEN wave goodbye to Grandmother.*) I was left alone with this new feeling of lightness and content.

JIMMY. I sat down in the middle of the garden (*ALL THREE sit, leaning on one anothers backs, shoulders or legs.*) where snakes could scarcely approach unseen. All about me giant grasshoppers, twice as big as any I had ever seen, were doing acrobatic feats among the dried vines.

JIM. The earth was warm under me, and warm as I crumbled it through my fingers.

JIMMY. (*After a pause.*) Nothing happened.

JIM. I did not expect anything to happen.

JAMES. I was something that lay under the sun and felt it, like the pumpkins, and I did not want to be anything more.

JIM, JAMES, JIMMY. I was entirely happy.

JIMMY. Perhaps we feel like that when we die . . .

JIM. . . . and become a part of something entire, whether it is sun and air, or goodness or knowledge.

JAMES. At any rate, that is happiness; to be dissolved into something complete and great.

JIM. When it comes to one, it comes as naturally as sleep.

## Act I
### Scene 4

### Sunflowers and the Shimerdas

*After a moment GRANDMOTHER and OTTO enter. THEY have loaded the wagon with supplies and provisions. The wagon is a small platform outfitted with a buckboard seat or bench. When GRANDMOTHER calls, JIMMY runs to OTTO who lifts him up onto the wagon seat. JAMES and JIM exit together.*

GRANDMOTHER. (*As OTTO assists her up and into the seat.*) Come along Jim, Otto is going to drive us over to make the acquaintance of our new Bohemian neighbors. They've come to live on a wild place where there's no garden or chicken house and very little broken land.

OTTO. (*Taking his place to drive the imaginary team.*) Come on Jimmy. Here we go.

JIMMY. The road ran about like a wild thing. And all along it, wherever it looped or ran, the sunflowers grew. They made a gold ribbon across the prairie.

OTTO. Them sunflowers were introduced into this country by the Mormons at the time of the persecution, when they left Missouri and struck out into the wilderness to find a place where they could worship God in their own way. The members of the first exploring party, crossing the plains to Utah scattered sunflower seed as they went.

The next summer, when the long trains of wagons came through with all the women and children, they had the sunflower trail to follow.

GRANDMOTHER. Now that may or may not be true, but sunflower bordered roads always seem to me the roads to freedom. Jimmy, this family bought Krajiek's place long before they left Bohemia—sight unseen—no idea it was worthless! That weasel Krajiek is the only person hereabouts can talk their language.

OTTO. I'm told the father is old and frail and knows nothing about farming. He used to be a tailor and fiddler, of all things.

GRANDMOTHER. If they're nice people, I hate to think of them spending the winter in that cave of Krajiek's, it's no better than a badger hole, not a proper dugout at all. And I hear he's made them pay twenty dollars for his old cookstove that ain't worth ten.

OTTO. (*Angry.*) Yes'm and he's sold 'em his oxen and his two bony old horses for the price of good workteams. I'd have interfered about the horses—the old man can understand some German—if I'd a thought it would do any good. I'm Austrian, you know, and Bohemians has a natural distrust of Austrians.

GRANDMOTHER. Now, why is that, Otto?

OTTO. Well, ma'm, it's politics. It would take me a long while to explain.

JIMMY. As we approached the Shimerdas' dwelling, I could still see nothing but rough red banks with long roots hanging out where the earth had crumbled away.

(*ANNIE races on from her work, SHE is barefoot.*)

ANNIE. (*In Czech.*) Come quickly everyone, it's Jimmy from the train. (*In English.*) It is Jimmy—Jimmy my friend of the train.

(*MRS. SHIMERDA runs from the house with YULKA holding onto her mother's skirt. THEY are followed by AMBROZ and MAREK. MAREK is frightened by the visitors and lies on the ground a few yards away.*)

MRS. SHIMERDA. Droubridrn! Droubridrn! Very glad! House no good, house no good!

GRANDMOTHER. (*Shouting.*) You'll get fixed up comfortable after while, Mrs. Shimerda; make good house.

JIMMY. My grandmother always spoke in a very loud tone to foreigners, as if they were deaf.

GRANDMOTHER. I am Emmaline Burden. We are your neighbors and we wanted you to have these provisions; potatoes, flour, sugar and here, a basket of baked goods.

MRS. SHIMERDA. (*Takes the bread loaves from the basket, smelling them and purring. In English.*) Much good! Much thank! Much good! (*In Czech she commands.*) Children, tell the woman thank you.

(*The CHILDREN echo their mother in English and Czech. MAREK darts toward Mrs. Burden holding up his webbed hands and crowing like a rooster.*)

MAREK. Hoo-hoo-hoo-hoo.

*(MRS. SHIMERDA shrieks in Czech as AMBROZ constrains his brother. KRAJIEK runs up from the barn.)*

MRS. SHIMERDA. Stop it, Marek! Stop now! This is a good woman. (*SHE turns to Krajiek, speaking in Czech.*) Tell them Marek will not hurt them. He was born afflicted. Sweet Jesus only knows why. Sweet Jesus.

*(AMBROZ subdues MAREK by forcing him to the ground. MAREK screams. AMBROZ and ANTONIA kneel to embrace him. As THEY rock him in their arms, his cries are subdued.)*

KRAJIEK. She wants me to tell you he won't hurt nobody, Mrs. Burden. He was born like that. The others are smart. Ambroz he make good farmer.

GRANDMOTHER. Mr. Krajiek, Mr. Burden and I will never stand by and let you cheat and misuse this poor family. The neighbors say you have not been truthful with these poor souls.

KRAJIEK. Now Mrs. Burden, I am doing everything in my power to help them. Haven't I turned my own home over to them completely? Your man here knows I'm sleeping out in that barn, denying my personal comfort, to be close by to help in every way possible. A fine Christian woman like yourself can see it ain't my fault they cain't farm or speak English, but as God sees me I'll try to teach them and help 'um get on.

*(MR. SHIMERDA enters from the house. HE is neatly dressed. Under his coat HE wears a knitted gray vest and*

*instead of a collar, a silk scarf of dark bronze-green, carefully crossed and held together by a red coral pin.)*

GRANDMOTHER. You see that you do, with no shortchanges!

KRAJIEK. Mrs. Burden, this is Mr. Shimerda, the father. *(In Czech.)* Mr. Shimerda, this lovely lady is Mrs. Burden, your neighbor.

*(MR. SHIMERDA kisses her hand, simply as an honest act of great respect and courtesy, without affectation.)*

MR. SHIMERDA. *(In Czech.)* Mrs. Burden, have you met my family? My wife, our Ambroz, Marek, my Antonia and our little Yulka.

*(While KRAJIEK translates and GRANDMOTHER introduces OTTO FUCHS who in turn greets the family all over again, ANTONIA takes JIMMY to a private spot DS. The OTHERS will exit silently as if Mrs. Shimerda was taking Grandmother to inspect the dugout.)*

ANNIE. Thank you, Jimmy. Tell me more words please. Talk the English.

*(ANTONIA now runs and points to various objects, taking JIMMY running with her in a happy game of discovery. JIMMY says the name of the object and she repeats the name carefully.)*

JIMMY. (*With ANNIE repeating each word.*) Grass—
Barn—Wagon—Roadway—Windmill—Sky.

(*ANNIE points to Jimmy's eyes.*)

JIMMY. Eyes.
ANNIE. Eyes. (*SHE points to his eyes again.*)
JIMMY. I just told you. Eyes.
ANNIE. No, no, Jimmy. (*SHE points to the sky.*)
JIMMY. I told you that too. Sky. Sky!
ANNIE. No, no. (*SHE makes a broad gesture to the
heavens then points again to his eyes. SHE points to her
own eyes, shaking her head "no."*)
JIMMY. (*After a pause.*) Oh you mean the color. Blue,
blue!
ANNIE. Blue sky. Blue eyes. (*SHE points to a ring on
her middle finger.*)
JIMMY. Ring. A gold ring. It's very pretty.
ANNIE. (*Removing the ring.*) Gold ring?, you take.
Yes, for you. Much thanks.
JIMMY. No, no Antonia, no. I can't take your ring.
MR. SHIMERDA. (*Calling.*) Antonia, Antonia.
ANNIE. Tatinek, Tatinek.

(*MR. SHIMERDA approaches them carrying two books.
The OTHERS follow. HE holds the books out toward
Jimmy.*)

JIMMY. No, no thank you. No more presents.
GRANDMOTHER. They are alphabet books, son. One
in English and one in Bohemian.
MR. SHIMERDA. Te-e-ach, te-e-ach my Antonia.

*(With calls of good-bye and thank you, the SHIMERDAS take the supplies and provisions off toward their dugout. KRAJIEK laughs and waves mightily as GRANDMOTHER, OTTO FUCHS and JIMMY cross far downstage. The LIGHTING isolates the three of them as THEY speak to the audience. The wagon unit is removed.)*

OTTO. During those first months the Shimerdas never went to town. Krajiek encouraged them in the belief that in Black Hawk they would somehow be mysteriously separated from their money. They hated Krajiek.

GRANDMOTHER. *(Leaning on her rattlesnake cane.)* They kept him in their hold and fed him for the same reason that the prairie dogs and brown owls house the rattlesnakes—because they did not know how to get rid of him.

## ACT I
### Scene 5

### The Watermelons

*The lights and sky brighten to a brilliant late August day. Two months have passed.*

ANNIE. Mrs. Burden, Good news. *(Clapping her hands in joy.)* Good News, Mrs. Burden!

GRANDMOTHER. How well you are speaking now, Antonia. (*Loud.*) English is getting better, Jim you must be a good teacher.

ANNIE. English no good, but Jimmy teach me every day. Good news, my papa find friends with Russian mans. Last night he take me for see, and I can (*Points to her head as JIMMY says "understand."*) very much talk. They from part of Russia where talk is very like Bohemie talk.

JIMMY. Do you mean the two Russians who live up by the big prairie dog town?

ANNIE. (*Standing on tiptoe to show how tall Pavel is, then waddling with puffy cheeks to show Peter's size.*) One like this, very, other fat like butter.

OTTO. (*Explaining to Grandmother.*) They are husking corn just now for the Widow Stephens. They get by making signs, cain't nobody pronounce their names but everybody says they're good farmhands.

JIMMY. Russia seems to me more remote than any other country—farther away than China, almost as far as the North Pole.

OTTO. Folks calls the thin one Pavel and the other Rosshian Peter.

ANNIE. We go now to meet them, Jimmy. You like and they like you. We talk English all the way.

JIMMY. May I Grandmother?

GRANDMOTHER. Are your chores done? All the eggs in from my henhouse?

JIMMY. Yes 'um.

GRANDMOTHER. Take Dude, now that Antonia has learned to double with you, so you won't be late for supper.

*(PETER enters far upstage bellowing a happy Russian drinking song. HE is pushing a wheelbarrow of melons, squashes and cucumbers. HE has a large corn knife and two grain sacks. PETER and the CHILDREN gather around the wheelbarrow.)*

PETER. (*Spoken mostly in Russian, but HE begins in broken English. The English phrases are in parentheses.*) (In my country rich peoples have cow.) (In America Peter have cow.) The milk is very good for my friend Pavel who is often sick. (Cow) is my greatest prize. But my melons are also fine. Eat.

ANNIE. (*Translating.*) Cow milk is good for his friend Pavel who is very much sick. His melons, as you see, are also fine. We must eat.

*(PETER uses his corn knife to begin, then HE starts cracking open melons against the side of the barrow. The CHILDREN and PETER laugh wildly as the melons smash. THEY eat melons with their hands, laughing.)*

PETER. (*In Russian.*) Melons better than medicine in Russia. If I could have stayed at home maybe now I have a fine daughter and a little son.

ANNIE. He says, melons better than medicine in Russia. If he stayed back home maybe he have girl and boy like us.

JIMMY. Why did he leave Russia?

ANNIE. (*In Czech.*) Why did you leave Russia?

*(PAVEL joins them. His sudden appearance is almost threatening.)*

PAVEL. *(Sternly, in Russian.)* Because of Great Trouble.

ANNIE. He says only because of great trouble.

PETER. *(In Russian, as HE prepares a bag of cucumbers for each child. His attitude has been changed by Pavel.)* Tell boy to have his grandmother cook them in milk as we do.

ANNIE. He says, you must tell your grandmother to cook these in milk as in old kawntree.

JIMMY. I've never heard of anybody cooking cucumbers at all.

ANNIE. Much good! Thank you! Peter, thank you!

*(ANNIE and JIMMY run off.*
*PETER stuffs more melon in his mouth as HE exits with the barrow.)*

## ACT I
### Scene 6

### Hop  Hop  Music

*TONY and ANTONIA enter briskly. JIMMY and ANNIE chase back on stage in a spirited game of tag. THEY race in circles around ANTONIA and TONY who cannot avoid becoming physically involved in the game as*

*THEY speak to the audience. ANNIE is, in spite of the cooler weather still barefoot. ANTONIA and TONY will stand on stage watching the scene with great empathy.*

ANTONIA. One afternoon we were having our reading lesson on the warm grassy bank where the badger lived. There was a shiver of coming winter in the air.

TONY. All those fall afternoons were the same, but I never got used to them.

*(JIMMY and ANNIE fall to the floor "catching" each other. THEY cannot stop laughing.)*

ANTONIA. We were extravagantly happy.

*(JIMMY is reading from a little book ANNIE has produced from her apron pocket. HE points to each word. SHE is shivering. HE holds her close for warmth.)*

JIMMY. Jessie James and his men often found it necessary to tramp along river banks hunting for deer and jack rabbits to cook at their camp fires.

ANNIE. Shh! Jimmy—singing—someone is singing.

JIMMY. I don't hear anything.

ANNIE. Quiet, listen. *(THEY search about them.)* Ah, here is music—little hop-hop—what you call?

JIMMY. Grasshopper—I thought the cold had killed them all off.

ANNIE. No, here is one Hop-Hop left—Come sing for me. We will keep you warm. *(SHE picks him up, warming the grasshopper in her hand. SHE begins singing a Bohemian lullaby to her new friend rocking him in her hands.*) I name this Hop hop "Old Hata" for the beggar woman in our village who sang to children in chirping voice, like this. We loved Old Hata and saved her our sweet cakes. (*SHE begins to cry.*)

JIMMY. Antonia, what's the matter?

ANNIE. Is all gone now, Jimmy. Our village, Old Hata, our life. (*SHE puts the grasshopper in her hair carefully with Jimmy's help.*)

JIMMY. We are starting new lives now together.

(*We hear a GUNSHOT offstage. BOTH CHILDREN are startled. MR. SHIMERDA enters with a gun and a stained sack, containing three rabbits.*)

MR. SHIMERDA. (*In Czech.*) My Antonia, I never intended to startle you.

(*HE opens his arms and ANTONIA runs to him. JIMMY follows.*)

MR. SHIMERDA. My hunting was good today, I get three. (*HE holds up three fingers, then says in English.*) How you call, Jimmy? Rabbits?

JIMMY. Rabbits.

MR. SHIMERDA. (*In Czech.*) I will make a winter hat from the skins for my Antonia.

ANNIE. My Tatinek make me a little hat with the skins, little hat for winter. Meat for eat, skin for hat.

(*MR. SHIMERDA starts to touch Annie's hair. SHE catches his wrist and lifts out the grasshopper, as THEY*

*move privately away from Jimmy. ANTONIA and
TONY also move to their father.)*

ANNIE. Is Hop-hop, Tatinek. (*In Czech.*) Like Old
Hata, remember? Listen, music. (*HE bends to listen.*)
Music.

MR. SHIMERDA. Mue - sic.

*(ANNIE sings the Bohemian lullaby for him. TONY and
ANTONIA join the song. ALL THREE implore their
father to sing and dance with them. MR. SHIMERDA
sings with them for a brief moment then can no longer
continue. HE moves from their arms to retrieve the
hunting sack and his gun.)*

MR. SHIMERDA. (*In Czech.*) Tell Jimmy when he is
a grown man I will give him this fine gun.

ANNIE. My Tatinek say when you are big boy, he give
you his gun. Very fine, from Bohemie. Great man give to
my papa for playing violin at wedding. Someday Papa give
you.

*(MR. SHIMERDA exits, sadly.)*

ANNIE. My papa sick all the time, he not look good. I
love my papa so, Jimmy.

*(ANNIE and JIMMY exit.)*

## ACT I
### Scene 7

### The Wolves

TONY. While the autumn color was growing pale on the grass and cornfields, things went badly with our friends the Russians. Peter told his troubles to father. He was unable to meet a note which fell due on the first of November; had to pay an exorbitant bonus on renewing it, and to give a mortgage on his pigs and horses and even his milk cow. His creditor was Wick Cutter the Black Hawk money lender.

ANTONIA. Soon after Peter renewed his note, Pavel strained himself lifting timbers for a new barn, and fell over among the shavings with such a gush of blood from the lungs that his fellow workmen thought he would die on the spot. They hauled him home and put him into his bed, and there he lay, very ill indeed. Misfortune seemed to settle like an evil bird on the roof of the log house, and to flap its wings there, warning human beings away.

*(During the narration, GRANDFATHER enters with a five-gallon milk can. MR. SHIMERDA and YULKA enter with a small canister to buy milk. PETER runs on speaking rapidly in Russian. GRANDMOTHER and JIMMY rush onstage.)*

PETER. *(In Russian.)* Please, please Mr. Shimerda, there has been an accident. Pavel is now coughing blood from his lungs. He begs for a priest to make confession. You must come at once.

ANNIE. (*Translating.*) There has been an accident. Pavel is hurt. He (*SHE mimes.*) spits the blood.

MR. SHIMERDA. (*In Czech.*) I am not a priest, but I will come at once.

*(MR. SHIMERDA gives YULKA the filled milk canister, finds a coin and pays Grandfather. YULKA runs off for home.)*

PETER. (*In Russian.*) Come now in my wagon.

ANNIE. He begs for priest for confession. There is none. Jimmy go with us.

JIMMY. Grandmother, may I go please?

GRANDMOTHER. Don't you get in the way, Jim Burden, and maybe you can be a help.

*(PETER runs far US followed by MR. SHIMERDA, ANNIE, JIMMY, ANTONIA and TONY. The Pavel bedroom quickly pivots onstage. PETER leads the other players as THEY circle above the set. PAVEL is standing in the bed screaming. The room is Spartan; a large ornate Russian crucifix dominates the other furnishings. A small handmade icon hangs near the entry door. Pavel's bed is long and narrow, made of wooden planks—not unlike a snow sledge. YULKA, GRANDFATHER and GRANDMOTHER run to their homes.)*

PAVEL. (*In Russian.*) Wolves! Wolves! Closer now. Save me Jesus. Sweet Mary stop the wolves.

ANNIE. It's the wolves, Jimmy, he is frightened by the wolves.

JIMMY. Those are coyotes on the ridge outside, not wolves.

*(PAVEL coughs violently, staining his shirt and bedclothes with blood that pours from his mouth. During the following dialogue, TONY and ANTONIA will enter and crouch with ANNIE and JIMMY.)*

PAVEL. *(In Russian.)* I must tell you, make confession.

TONY. He begs for a priest.

MR. SHIMERDA. *(In Czech.)* I am not a priest but I am your friend.

ANNIE. My Tatinek not priest, but will listen as friend.

PAVEL. *(In Russian.)* I must tell.

PETER. Nyet! Nyet! Nyet!

PAVEL. *(In Russian.)* Will you hear me?

MR. SHIMERDA. *(In Czech.)* Yes my friend, I will listen.

PETER. Nyet! Nyet! Nyet!

JIMMY. Antonia then began to translate the sick man's confession. We were to speak of nothing else for weeks.

ANTONIA. Years later, we still marveled at the story. I have never forgotten the passion of these two men, locked together for a lifetime, intimately, in a relationship not of affection, but of disgrace.

*(In the following PAVEL speaks in first person tense, in Russian. Pavel's complete text appears in the dialogue language glossary. ANTONIA, ANNIE and TONY in third person, in English. PAVEL begins his story*

*simply—even playfully. HE and PETER "relive" the*
*story with them. Pavel's Russian phrases must always*
*precede the English translation. However, because of the*
*structure of the two languages, PAVEL and the*
*ANTONIAS may often mirror the same gestures.*
*Pavel's Russian speeches are scripted in the glossary.*
*His story flows forward never seeming to be aware of*
*the translation. The Russian often becomes a deep*
*baritone background for the women's English phrases*
*on top.*
PAVEL *begins his confession in Russian.)*

ANNIE. When Pavel and Peter were young men, living
at home in Russia, they were asked to be groomsmen for a
friend who was to marry the belle of another village.

TONY. It was in the dead of winter and the groom's
party went over to the wedding in sledges. Peter and Pavel
drove in the groom's sledge, and six sledges followed with
all his relatives and friends. After the ceremony at the
church, the party went to a dinner given by the parents of
the bride. The dinner lasted all afternoon; then it became a
supper and continued far into the night.

ANNIE. There was much dancing and drinking. At
midnight the parents of the bride said goodbye to her and
blessed her.

ANTONIA. The groom took her up in his arms and
carried her out to his sledge and tucked her under the
blankets. He sprang in beside her, and Pavel and
Peter . . .

JIMMY. *Our* Pavel and Peter?

ANTONIA, ANNIE & TONY. YES!

ANTONIA. . . . took the front seat. Pavel drove. The party set out with singing and the jingle of sleigh bells, the groom's sledge going first. All the drivers were more or less the worse for merry-making, and the groom was absorbed in his bride.

TONY. The wolves were bad that winter, and everyone knew it, yet when they heard the first wolf cry, the drivers were not much alarmed. They had too much good food and drink inside them. The first howls were taken up and echoed with quickening repetitions.

ANNIE. The wolves were coming together.

ANTONIA. There was no moon, but the starlight was clear on the snow. A black drove came up over the hill behind the wedding party. The wolves ran like streaks of shadow; they looked no bigger than dogs, but there were hundreds of them. Something happened to the hindmost sledge: the driver lost control—he was probably very drunk—the horses left the road, the sledge was caught in a clump of trees, and overturned. The occupants rolled out over the snow, and the fleetest of the wolves sprang upon them.

TONY. The shrieks that followed made everybody sober. The drivers stood up and lashed their horses. The groom had the best team and his sledge was the lightest— all the others carried from six to a dozen people.

*(PAVEL stands in the bed and lashes the imagined troika before him.)*

ANTONIA. Another driver lost control. The screams of the horses were more terrible to hear than the cries of the men and women. Nothing seemed to check the wolves. It was hard to tell what was happening in the rear; the people who were falling behind shrieked as piteously as those who were already lost.

*(PAVEL sits on the wooden headboard.)*

TONY. The little bride hid her face on the groom's shoulder and sobbed. Pavel sat still and watched his horses. The road was clear and white, and the groom's three blacks went like the wind. It was only necessary to be calm and to guide them carefully. At length, as they breasted a long hill, Peter rose cautiously and looked back. "There are only three sledges left," he whispered. "And the wolves?" Pavel asked.

PETER and ANNIE. *(In Russian.)* Enough! Enough for all of us!

TONY. Pavel reached the brow of the hill, but only two sledges followed him down the other side. In that moment on the hilltop, they saw behind them a whirling black group on the snow. Presently the groom screamed. He saw his father's sledge overturned, with his mother and sisters. He sprang up as if he meant to jump, but the girl shrieked and held him back.

ANTONIA. It was even then too late. The black ground-shadows were already crowding over the heap in the road, and one horse ran out across the fields, his harness hanging to him, wolves at his heels.

TONY. But the groom's movement had given Pavel an idea. They were within a few miles of their village now. The only sledge left out of six was not very far behind them, and Pavel's middle horse was failing. Beside a frozen pond something happened to the other sledge; Peter saw it plainly. Three big wolves got abreast of the horses, and the horses went crazy. They tried to jump over each other, got tangled up in the harness, and overturned the sledge.

ANTONIA. When the shrieking behind them died away, Pavel realized that he was alone upon the familiar road. "They still come?" he asked Peter.

ANNIE and PETER. "Yes."

TONY. "How many?"

ANNIE and PETER. "Twenty, thirty—enough."

TONY. Enough.

ANTONIA. Now his middle horse was being almost dragged by the other two. Pavel gave Peter the reins and stepped carefully into the back of the sledge. He called to the groom that they must lighten—and pointed to the bride.

*(PAVEL points to Annie. SHE screams. PETER and MR. SHIMERDA lunge to restrain Pavel.)*

TONY. The young man cursed him and held her tighter.

ANTONIA. Pavel tried to drag her away.

TONY. In the struggle, the groom rose.

ANTONIA. Pavel knocked him over the side of the sledge and threw the girl after him.

*(PAVEL throws MR. SHIMERDA to the floor. ANNIE runs to him. PETER kneels at the foot of the bed. PAVEL resumes his place, seated on the headboard.)*

TONY. He never remembered exactly how he did it, or what happened afterward.

ANNIE. Peter, crouching in the front seat, saw nothing.

ANTONIA. The first thing either of them noticed was a new sound that broke into the clear air, . . .

ALL THREE ANTONIAS. . . . louder than they had ever heard before—the bell of the monastery of their own village, ringing for early prayers.

*(We hear the sound of the MONASTERY BELL, loudly. EVERYONE in the room covers their ears in pain to shut out the tolling of God's reprimand. PAVEL throws himself to his knees in the center of the bed.)*

PAVEL and ANTONIA. Pavel and Peter drove into the village alone, and they have been alone ever since. They were run out of their village. Pavel's own mother would not look at him. They went away to strange towns, but when people learned where they came from, they were always asked if they knew the two men who had fed the bride to the wolves. Wherever they went, the story followed them. It took them five years to save money enough to come to America. They worked in Chicago, Des Moines, Fort Wayne, but they were always unfortunate. When Pavel's health grew so bad, they decided to try farming.

*(PETER and MR. SHIMERDA tenderly cover Pavel's sleeping body. JIMMY and THE ANTONIAS step toward the audience as Pavel's bedroom pivots offstage.)*

JIMMY. Pavel died a few days after he unburdened his mind to Mr. Shimerda, and was buried in the Norwegian graveyard.

ANNIE. Peter sold off everything, and left the country.

TONY. And went to be a cook in the railway construction camp where gangs of Russians were employed.

ANTONIA. The loss of his two friends had a devastating effect on my papa from which he never, never recovered.

## ACT I
### Scene 8

### Visit to the Dugout

*The Burden Wagon—GRANDMOTHER and GRANDFATHER enter with OTTO and JAKE. THEY have a large food hamper and a crate of woolen clothes and blankets. THEY are dressed for the cold— GRANDMOTHER in her full-length hooded green cape.*

OTTO. Yes m'am, they need every bit of these woolen goods your church ladies collected.

GRANDMOTHER. (*As GRANDFATHER helps her step up into the wagon.*) It has turned decidedly cold. Josiah was just saying the wind was whipping at us straight from Alaska.

OTTO. Folks say, they ain't got but one overcoat amongst 'em, and they takes turns wearing it.

JAKE. All 'cept for the crazy boy. He never wears the coat but he's turrible strong.

OTTO. Somehow, afflicted people seem to be able to stand most anything.

GRANDMOTHER. God bless his dear soul.

*(JIMMY, in a heavy coat, runs to the wagon. GRANDFATHER boosts him up to the seat next to Grandmother.)*

JAKE They'll sho' love all this food 'cause rabbits must be gettin' scarce in this locality.

JIMMY. What do you mean about rabbits?

JAKE That Ambroz come along by the cornfield yesterday up where I was a workin' and showed me three prairie dogs he'd shot. He asked me if they was good to eat.

*(HE acts out his response, with spitting and comic faces. JIMMY laughs.)*

JAKE. I spit and made a face or two—just took on, to scare him, but he just stood there looking like he was smarter'n me and stuffed them prairie dogs back in his sack and walked on off.

*(JAKE and OTTO laugh heartily as JAKE seats himself in the drivers seat.)*

GRANDMOTHER. Josiah, you don't suppose Krajiek would let them poor creatures eat prairie dogs, do you?

GRANDFATHER. Emmaline that's what you are braving this weather to find out.

OTTO. Prairie dogs are clean beasts and ought to be good for food, but their family connections are against them.

JIMMY. What do you mean?

OTTO. Well, Jim, they belong to the rat family.
JAKE. (*To the horses.*) Up—we—go.

(*GRANDFATHER and OTTO move away from the wagon.*)

GRANDMOTHER. (*Standing in the bumping wagon to call instructions.*) Otto, if you can find that old rooster that got his comb froze, just give his neck a twist, and bring him along—follow us on up there, on Thor.

(*JIMMY and JAKE help her sit down.*)

GRANDMOTHER. There's no good reason why Mrs. Shimerda couldn't have got hens from her neighbors last summer and had a hen house going by now. I reckon she was confused and didn't know where to begin. I've come strange to a new country myself, but I never forgot hens are a good thing to have, no matter what you don't have.
JAKE. Just as you say, ma'm, but I hate to think of Krajiek getting a leg of that old rooster.

(*The Shimerda's dugout interior pivots to position. A small crude cook stove provides the less than meager warmth. One smoky oil lamp sits on a rickety table. There are crates and a small barrel near the entry. MRS. SHIMERDA has pulled the only chair to the stove and sits there weeping. MAREK lies at her feet like a big dog. MR. SHIMERDA and YULKA huddle on a small tin trunk which has been placed at the foot of Mrs. Shimerda's bed, which is unseen. ANNIE approaches her father carrying his beautiful wooden violin case*

*from Bohemia. The SHIMERDAS have wrapped their*
*feet and lower legs in rags for warmth.)*

ANNIE. (*In Czech.*) Play for us, Tatinek. A fine song
for dancing the Polka. (*In English.*) Yulka, dance with me.
Papa, make the music, we will dance the Polka. (*HE takes
the case cradling it in his arms like a new born child for the
remainder of the scene.*) Come, Yulka.

*(The GIRLS begin jumping up and down. MAREK howls
sensing the arrival of the Burdens. JIMMY, JAKE and
GRANDMOTHER climb from the wagon carrying their
gifts. MRS. SHIMERDA rises and runs out from the
room toward the wagon.)*

ANNIE. Dance with us, Mamenka, music, Papa please.

*(MRS. SHIMERDA drags GRANDMOTHER inside.
KRAJIEK arrives, running from the barn. JAKE and
JIMMY will not allow him to help them carry in the
supplies. AMBROZ runs into the dugout wearing a
large hat and the family overcoat. HE carries the
hunting gun. JAKE, with the crate and JIMMY, with
the food hamper follow AMBROZ. KRAJIEK crouches
near the entry. The wagon is withdrawn.)*

MRS. SHIMERDA. (*In Czech and broken English—
English words are marked in parenthesis.*) (We freeze.) At
last you've come. (Is no food). Mr. Shimerda is worthless,
he can find no game hunting all day. [*Pounding on Ambroz
chest.]* (Ambroz kills rats. I not cook them rats). Why did
God send us to this (hell place?) No coats, no shoes. We

wear rags for shoes in this hell place. Look Mrs. Burden, potatoes are frozen, weevils have eaten the flour. (Krajiek talk lies—lies.) [*SHE snatches up an empty coffee pot from the stove and shakes it in Mrs. Burden's face.*] (We got nothing, nothing.) [*SHE falls to the floor sobbing.*]

GRANDMOTHER. (*Very loud, as JIMMY and JAKE place the hamper and crate on the table.*) Yes, Mrs. Shimerda, things are bad now but you wait till spring. You'll get things sorted out nicely. Antonia, my dear, come help me unpack these few things.

ANNIE. You not mind my poor mamenka, Mrs. Burden. She is so sad.

(*As the food is unpacked MAREK begins barking like a dog and pounces toward the food. AMBROZ subdues him then strokes him lovingly and rocks him. JAKE brings in a large bag of potatoes.*)

GRANDMOTHER. Haven't you got any sort of cave or cellar outside, Antonia? This is no place to keep vegetables. How did your potatoes get frozen?

ANNIE. We get from Mr. Bushy, at the post office— what he throw out. We got no potatoes, Mrs. Burden.

(*MR. SHIMERDA stands, takes a lantern and motions Mrs. Burden to step behind the stove. HE holds the lamp towards a small dark hole or cave behind the stove. There is some light bedding in the cave. HE speaks in English as HE holds the lantern into the tiny cave.*)

MR. SHIMERDA. My Yulka, My Antonia.

GRANDMOTHER. You mean they sleep in there? Your girls?

MR. SHIMERDA. (*Nods sadly, then embraces Ambroz.*) Me—my sons—sleeps—with ox—in barn.

ANNIE. (*SHE and her sister crawl into the little cave.*) Is very cold on floor, this is warm. I like for sleep here. My mamenka have nice bed, with pillows from our own geese in Bohemie. See, Jim?

GRANDMOTHER. You'll have a better house after while, Antonia, and then you will forget these hard times. In this crate we brought along some blankets and woolen clothes, the Widow Stephens will bring out boots and shoes for all of you.

(*MR. SHIMERDA makes GRANDMOTHER sit on the only chair. HE lifts Mrs. Shimerda to the trunk. HE and the children surround her. THEY all face Grandmother.*)

MR. SHIMERDA. (*In English, forcefully.*) We not beggars—never beggars—we build house in spring. Ambroz will someday be rich with much land—good life.

AMBROZ. (*In English.*) We build new house in spring.

ANNIE. Tatinek and Ambroz have already split the logs for it, but the logs were all buried in the snow.

MRS. SHIMERDA. (*In English.*) You much good woman. I lose my head, please forgive. (*SHE kneels and kisses grandmother's hands.*) Dear Mrs. Burden.

GRANDMOTHER. (*Standing.*) Mrs. Shimerda, please stop this at once. We can all understand your distress.

(*MRS. SHIMERDA opens the tin trunk, laughing frantically and removes a long bag made of bed ticking.*)

*SHE measures out a cupful of the shavings inside and ties them in a cloth SHE has placed in Grandmother's hand.)*

MRS. SHIMERDA. (*In English.*) For cook. Little now, be very much when cook.

*(MAREK smacks his lips and rubs his tummy.)*

MRS. SHIMERDA. Very good, you no have in this country. All things better for eat in my country.
GRANDMOTHER. Maybe so, Mrs. Shimerda.
ANNIE. Cook with rabbit, cook with chicken, in the gravy. Oh so good!

*(The SHIMERDAS call out Thank yous in Czech and English as GRANDMOTHER, JAKE and JIMMY hurry toward the wagon. JIM BURDEN joins them.)*

KRAJIEK. Bless you dear lady. You are everything the Bible teaches us a Christian should be! (*HE exits following the dugout as it pivots off.)*
GRANDMOTHER. (*Standing downstage.*) What's a body to do, Jake? Where do you begin with these people? They're wanting in everything and most of all in horse sense. Nobody can give them that.
JIMMY. What did she give you, Grandmother?
GRANDMOTHER. (*Opening the small bundle.*) I have no earthly idea.
JAKE. They might be dried meat from some queer beast, Jim. They ain't dried fish, and they never grew on stalk or vine. I'm afraid of 'em.

GRANDMOTHER. Anyhow I don't want to eat anything that had been shut up for months with old clothes and goose pillows.

*(GRANDMOTHER, JAKE and JIMMY share a good laugh as THEY exit.)*

JIM. She threw the package into the stove, but I bit off a corner of one of the chips I held in my hand, and chewed it tentatively. I never forgot the strange taste; though it was many years before I knew that those little brown shavings, which the Shimerdas had brought so far and treasured so jealously, were dried mushrooms. They had been gathered, probably, in some deep Bohemian forest. *(HE exits.)*

## ACT I
### Scene 9

### Christmas Day

*The Burden kitchen pivots on. The wash tub has been removed and a small side table added. On this table is a little evergreen decorated for Christmas. OTTO, GRANDMOTHER and JAKE are adding the finishing touches. GRANDFATHER and JIMMY enter.*

GRANDFATHER. I feel badly, son, that the snow has been so heavy that we could not get to town for the purchases you and your grandmother had wanted, but she said we can have our own country Christmas without any help from town. Jake was telling me that he and your father would cut one of these little cedar trees each year as I had done, back in Virginia. I've kept my eye on this little feller for several months now, over on Squaw Creek. Merry Christmas, Jimmy.

JIMMY. Oh Grandfather, thank you, it's beautiful.

*(GRANDFATHER lights his pipe and settles in his chair. During the following speeches THEY will complete the decorations for the tree.)*

JAKE. Help me with this popcorn, Jimmy. Otto's done fitted these little candles into pasteboard sockets.

GRANDMOTHER. Have you ever seen such beautiful angels? Otto had these in his old cowboy trunk.

OTTO. My mother, back in Vienna, has sent these various figures to me year after year. And as you know Mrs. Burden I never let a Christmas day pass without writing her a long, long letter in German, no matter where I am. Though it gets tougher each year to remember the words, I've got so used to talking English.

JIMMY. (*Pointing to figures on the tree.*) Here's a camel and a Shepherd and wise men.

JAKE. What's this 'un?

JIMMY. That looks like a wild panther.

JAKE. I don't remember panthers in the baby Jesus story.

JIMMY. Well, maybe we'll have to make up some new stories with wild panthers. Can't we Grandfather?

GRANDFATHER. I suppose so, son. With all these stories we may have a brand new "tree of knowledge."

*(THEY laugh.)*

JIMMY. At about four o'clock a visitor appeared: Mr. Shimerda.

MR. SHIMERDA. *(Enters wearing his rabbit skin collar and cap.)* Forgive my come. I want thank you for nice things you do for Shimerdas. Much, much nice things

*(GRANDFATHER stands, shakes his hand and brings him to a chair next to his at the table.)*

GRANDMOTHER. *(Placing the decanter and glasses on the table.)* You must join us in a glass of Virginia apple brandy. Otto, kindly dip Jimmy a root beer. *(SHE serves the brandy, then says loudly.)* We say Merry Christmas today.

MR. SHIMERDA. *(HE repeats, in English.)* Merry Christmas. *(Then in Czech.)* Merry Christmas.

*(THEY all try to repeat the Czech phrase. Laughing with them, JIM BURDEN steps into the scene standing US of Jimmy's chair. During the following OTTO will try to explain as much as he can to Mr. Shimerda in German.)*

MR. SHIMERDA. Thank you. Thank you.

*(GRANDMOTHER speaks very loudly as OTTO struggles along, translating in German.)*

GRANDMOTHER. What a fine hat and collar. I bet you made these yourself. You know, Mr. Shimerda, all of us, your neighbors admire the lovely way you fold that beautiful cravat and always the stick pin, fixed just so. We never saw a man keep himself so nice.

MR. SHIMERDA. *(In German, for Otto to translate in English.)* Thank you, Mrs. Burden. Your home is so beautiful it quite takes my heart. Things seem so far removed from me now that I am so far away.

JIM. I suppose, in the crowded clutter of their cave, the old man had come to believe that peace and order had vanished from the earth. His face had a look of weariness and pleasure, like that of sick people when they feel relief from pain.

MR. SHIMERDA. *(Rising, speaking in German—no translation.)* I must not overstay my time. What is this?

JIMMY. Oh Mr. Shimerda that's our Christmas tree. Grandfather may we light the candles now before Mr. Shimerda has to go home?

*(GRANDFATHER nods permission. OTTO begins singing "Silent Night" in German. OTTO and JAKE light the candles. MR. SHIMERDA crosses himself and reverently kneels at the tree, pulling his body into a tight "S.")*

GRANDMOTHER. I worried about Josiah. He was rather narrow in religious matters, and sometimes spoke out and hurt people's feelings. There had been nothing strange about the tree before, but now, with someone kneeling before it—images, candles . . . Josiah merely

put his finger-tips to his brow and bowed his head, thus
Protestantizing the atmosphere.

MR. SHIMERDA. (*Crosses himself, stands and makes
the sign of the cross above Jimmy's head.*) Good wo-man.
Danke! Danke!

(*OTTO holds up a lantern. MR. SHIMERDA exits into
the dark evening, US with the lantern. OTTO and JAKE
extinguish the candles and after Grandfather's line,
THEY remove the side table and tree.*)

GRANDFATHER. The prayers, Jimmy, of all good
people are good.

(*JIM BURDEN, GRANDFATHER, JAKE and OTTO exit
into the darkness as JAMES enters.*)

## ACT I
### Scene 10

### Mrs. Shimerda's Visit

JAMES. (*Carries in a bench which HE places where the
Christmas tree had been, as HE completes his narration.*)
The week following Christmas brought in a thaw, and by
New Year's Day all the world about us was a broth of gray
slush. During this interval of fine weather, Antonia and her
mother rode over on one of their shaggy old horses to pay
us a visit. It was the first time Mrs. Shimerda had been to
our house.

*(ANNIE and MRS. SHIMERDA have arrived, carefully stepping over the frozen puddles.)*

GRANDMOTHER. Why Antoniä! Mrs. Shimerda! How lovely you've come over. We'll have some fruitcake and tea.

MRS. SHIMERDA. *(Almost running about the kitchen, speaking rapidly in Czech. English phrases are in parenthesis.)* Mrs. Burden, such a fine house you have. (Look at stove, very nice.) I had a beautiful kitchen and a house much better than this in Bohemia. Better curtains, better furniture. I give up everything (so my Ambroz be a rich man in America someday) and he will, even if I must (live like badger in filthy cave) with nothing. [*SHE picks up an iron pot from the top of the stove*] You got many, Shimerdas no got.

GRANDMOTHER. Then you must take that pan along with you. Now won't you have a cup of tea with me?

*(GRANDMOTHER holds back a chair for MRS. SHIMERDA who sits clutching her pot. GRANDMOTHER will pour cups of tea, then sit with her.)*

MRS. SHIMERDA. You got many things for cook. If I got all things like you, I make much better.

GRANDMOTHER. Yes. Well now, this fruitcake is from our recipe back in Virginia. Things were quite different for me back in Virginia, I must say.

*(ANNIE and JIMMY separate themselves to study an alphabet book which ANNIE carries to the bench.)*

ANNIE. My papa sad for old country. He don't like this kawntree!

JIMMY. (*Angry.*) People who don't like this country ought to stay at home. We don't make them come here.

ANNIE. My papa not want to come, never! He cry for leave his old friends what make music with him. He love very much the man what play the long horn like this. (*SHE mimes a slide trombone.*) They go to school together and are friends from boys. But my mama, she want Ambroz for be rich, with many cattle.

JIMMY. (*Shouting.*) Your mama wants other people's things.

ANNIE. (*Shouting.*) Your grandfather is rich. Why he not help my papa?

GRANDMOTHER. (*Very loud, SHE stands.*) Once this frightful winter breaks, Mrs. Shimerda, I promise you we'll get all the menfolk here abouts over to your place and give Mr. Shimerda and Ambroz a hand with that log house he has planned. You'll be into your new house by spring and all ready for planting season. Everything is going to be much better for you by the time summer gets here.

MRS. SHIMERDA. (*Standing.*) House. Be good!

JIMMY. Grandfather says we should have an early spring, nice and dry so the corn won't be held back by too much rain as it was last year.

MRS. SHIMERDA. He not Jesus, he not know about the wet and dry.

JIMMY. Grandmother and I stood stock still, we did not answer her. What was the use?

MRS. SHIMERDA. (*Wrapping the remaining cake in one of Grandmother's kitchen napkins and stuffing it into the pot.*) Much thank you for the cake and the cookpot. Much good.

ANNIE. (*Kissing Grandmother.*) I will tell Papa about men working to build log house. Good news will make him happy. Yes, Tatinek will be happy and hopeful. We all try to be happy.

(*MRS. SHIMERDA and ANTONIA leave pleasantly with bows and thank yous to Grandmother.*)

JIMMY. I hope that snooping old woman won't come to see us anymore.

GRANDMOTHER. She's not old Jim, though I expect she seems old to you. No, I wouldn't mourn if she never came again. But a body never knows what traits poverty might bring out in 'em. It makes a woman grasping to see her children want for things. Now read me a chapter in "The Prince in the House of David." Let's forget the Bohemians.

## ACT I
### Scene 11

### Mr. Shimerda's Death

*JAMES runs downstage below the kitchen. GRANDMOTHER and JIMMY adjust properties. AMBROZ is aided to the bench by OTTO and JAKE. GRANDFATHER enters in his Sunday suit.*

JAMES. The biggest blizzard of the year began on my birthday. The snow did not fall this time, it spilled out of heaven like thousands of feather beds being emptied.

JIMMY. The next morning before I opened my eyes I seemed to know that something had happened.

GRANDMOTHER. (*Going between the stove and table.*) Oh dear Savior! Lord, thou knowest.

(*OTTO and JAKE help her with plates, coffee mugs or whatever is needed.*)

GRANDFATHER. (*To Jimmy as GRANDMOTHER continues repeating her prayers.*) Jimmy we will not have prayers this morning, because we have a great deal to do. Old Mr. Shimerda is dead, and his family are in great distress. Ambroz came over here in the middle of the night and Jake and Otto went back with him. The boys have had a hard night, and you must not bother them with questions. That is Ambroz, asleep on the bench. Come in to breakfast, boys.

(*THEY all sit in their accustomed places. The following lines must be read with mounting enthusiasm. This is a thrilling morning. The unbelievable has happened. Throughout THEY never stop eating.*)

GRANDFATHER. (*To Otto.*) Did no one hear the gunshot blast?

OTTO. (*Standing to get the coffee. HE pours mugs for everyone.*) No sir, nobody heard the gun go off. Ambroz was out with the ox team, trying to break a road, and the women-folks was shut up tight in their cave. When Ambroz come in the barn, it was dark and he didn't see nothing, but the oxen acted kind of queer. One of 'em ripped around and got away from him—bolted clean out of the stable. His hands is blistered where the rope run through. He got a lantern and went back and found the old man, just as we seen him. (*HE sits.*)

GRANDMOTHER. (*Remembering biscuits in the oven which SHE retrieves and serves round.*) Poor soul, poor soul! I'd like to think he never done it. He was always considerate and un-wishful to give trouble. How could he forget himself and bring this on us. (*SHE sits.*)

OTTO. I don't think he was out of his head for a minute, Mrs. Burden. He done everything natural. You know he was always sort of fixy, and fixy he was to the last. (*HE stands to demonstrate.*) When we found him, everything was decent except . . . except what he couldn't nowise foresee. His coat was hung on a peg, and his boots was under the bed. He'd took off that silk neckcloth he always wore, and folded it smooth and stuck his pin through it. He turned back his shirt at the neck and rolled up his sleeves. (*HE sits.*)

GRANDMOTHER. I don't see how he could do it!

OTTO. (*Stands again to act it out.*) Why, ma'm, it was simple enough; he pulled the trigger with his big toe! (*GRANDMOTHER shouts and clutches her stomach.*) He laid over on his side and put the end of the barrel in his mouth, then he drew up one foot and felt for the trigger. He found it all right! (*HE sits.*) Yes m'am.

JAKE. (*Rising mysteriously, while slopping strawberry jam on his biscuit.*) Maybe he did. There's something mighty queer about it.

GRANDMOTHER. Now what do you mean, Jake?

JAKE. Well, ma'm I found Krajiek's axe under the manger, and I picks it up and carries it over to the corpse, and I take my oath it just fit the gash in the front of the old man's face. That there Krajiek had been sneakin' round, pale and quiet, and when he seen me examinin' the axe, he begun whimperin', "My God, man, don't do that!" "I reckon I'm a-goin' to look into this," says I. Then he begun to squeal like a rat and run about wringin' his hands. "They'll hang me!" says he. "My God, they'll hang me sure!"

OTTO. (*Shouting as HE jumps up.*) Krajiek's gone silly, Jake, and so have you. The old man wouldn't have made all them preparations for Krajiek to murder him, would he? It don't hang together. The gun was right beside him when Ambroz found him.

JAKE. Krajiek could'a put it there, couldn't he?

GRANDMOTHER. See here, Jake Marpole, don't you go trying to add murder to suicide. We're deep enough in trouble. Otto reads you too many of them detective stories.

(*BOTH MEN sit sheepishly.*)

GRANDFATHER. It will be easy to decide all that Emmaline. If he shot himself the way they think, the gash will be torn from the inside outward.

OTTO. Just so it is, Mr. Burden. I seen bunches of hair and stuff sticking to the poles and straw along the roof. (*GRANDMOTHER yells with another stomach attack.*) They was blown up there by gunshot, no question.

GRANDMOTHER. (*Rises abruptly.*) Why that poor boy! I have completely forgotten myself. (*SHE quickly moves to Ambroz.*) Now Ambroz, you must take some nourishment before going back into that storm.

(*AMBROZ rolls to his knees, making the sign of the cross and clutching his rosary. SHE motions for help. SHE and JAKE help him to the table but HE continues his prayers, crossing himself repeatedly.*)

GRANDMOTHER. Now this is most frightful, but you must remain strong and healthy for your dear mother.

AMBROZ. (*In Czech.*) No, I must pray! Pray for my poor father in torment. I must pray for many years until Father flies from purgatory.

OTTO. He must pray for many years for his father's soul in purgatory. He believes his father is in great torment.

JIMMY. (*Loudly.*) I don't believe it!

(*The OTHERS are stunned.*)

GRANDMOTHER. Son! That's not for us to say.

JIMMY. It was homesickness that killed Mr. Shimerda. I think his spirit may be resting here with us, now warm by our stove, before making that long journey over the water to his old country.

GRANDFATHER. James, such things are not for us to say. Only our Lord knows.

AMBROZ. (*Suddenly, struggling with English.*) Must find please a priest. Tatinek must no die with no priest. Please find priest.

GRANDFATHER. I know of only one priest for this part of the territory and he's stationed out in the Irish town of O'Neil some two hundred miles west. (*Kneeling with his arm around Ambroz.*) Son, we will do all we possibly can but with the blizzard we've endured it will take several days to open the wagon road from our home to your mother's.

OTTO. (*In German, to Ambroz.*) Where do you want your father buried?

AMBROZ. (*Standing, shouting in broken English.*) Father must buried at crossroads. On my land. (*Making a crossroads with his arms.*) Where my land do this. Must be!

(*GRANDFATHER comforts him and eases him back into his chair where HE dives into breakfast.*)

GRANDMOTHER. I never heard of such a thing. He can rest in the Norwegian cemetery.

JAKE. No m'am, beg pardon, but them Norwegian Church Officers will have to hold a special meeting and they'll no sooner take in a suicide than the Catholics will.

GRANDMOTHER. If these foreigners are so clannish, we'll have to have an American graveyard that will be more liberal minded. I'll get right after you, Josiah, to start one in the spring. If anything was to happen to me I don't want the Norwegians holding inquisitions over me to see whether or not I'm good enough to be laid amongst them.

JAKE. No matter where he's buried we got ta' fix him up a box.

GRANDMOTHER. In this snow we'll never get an already made coffin here from Omaha.

JAKE. Old Otto can make us one. He's the best carpenter I ever see'd.

GRANDFATHER. You are a fine carpenter Fuchs, but have you ever made a coffin?

OTTO. The last time I made one of those, sir, was for a fellow in the Black Tiger Mine up above Silverton, Colorado. The mouth of that mine goes right into the face of the cliff, and they used to put us in a bucket and run us over on a trolley and shoot us into the shaft. The bucket traveled across a box canyon three hundred feet deep and about a third full of water. Two Swedes had fell out of that bucket once, and hit the water, feet down. If you'll believe it, they went to work the next day. You can't kill a Swede. (*THEY share a big laugh.*) But in my time a little Eyetalian tried the high dive, and it turned out different with him. We was snowed in then, like we are now, and I happened to be the only man in camp that could make a coffin for him. It's a handy thing to know, when you knock about like I've done.

GRANDMOTHER. We'd be hard put to it now, if you didn't know, Otto.

GRANDFATHER. Will you begin building a box for us, Fuchs? You may use that planking I was holding to re-floor the oat bin this spring. Because of the cold you may need to bring your bench and tools in here to stay warm.

*(The Burden kitchen now pivots offstage as AMBROZ exits stage right and the OTHERS stage left. The entire space becomes a wintery field. ANTONIA and TONY enter downstage right embracing one another. THEY do not wear coats. JIM BURDEN and JAMES enter from downstage left without coats. The MEN wrap their arms around each others shoulders. During the following narration, JAKE, OTTO, KRAJIEK and GRANDFATHER will enter upstage bundled in heavy coats, carrying a newly made pine coffin placed on simple wooden sawhorses. The coffin is positioned over*

*a center stage trap. THEY also carry two long lengths of heavy rope. The ropes are then threaded under the coffin and the excess roping is coiled neatly and hung on each sawhorse end.)*

ANTONIA. Papa lay dead in the barn four days and on the fifth we buried him. Ambroz and Mr. Burden chose a corner of high ground at the crossroads of our property.

JIM. Grandfather was fearful that when roadways were built they might intersect at that exact spot.

TONY. Mercifully the surveyors placed the roadways a few yards to the south.

ANTONIA. All day Friday Jake was off with Ambroz and Marek digging the grave, chopping out the frozen earth with old axes.

JAMES. On Saturday we breakfasted before daylight and got into the wagon with the coffin. Jake and Otto went on horseback to cut the body loose from the pool of blood in which it was frozen fast to the ground.

TONY. We bandaged his head in a clean white cloth.

*(ANTONIA and TONY begin singing the Bohemian lullaby as THEY slip off stage right. JAMES and JIM BURDEN exit downstage left. As JIMMY, dressed for winter, enters down left with GRANDMOTHER in her cape and hood, ANNIE in her rabbit fur cap and coat runs in from far upstage right. SHE races to embrace Jimmy.)*

ANNIE. Oh, Jimmy, what you think for my lovely papa! He kiss me and hold me so tight, then say he go hunt rabbits. You never forget my lovely papa, Jimmy? Never! You promise?

JIMMY. It seemed to me that I could feel her heart breaking as she clung to me.

*(MRS. SHIMERDA, AMBROZ, MAREK and YULKA enter from upstage right. EVERYONE stands shivering in the cold. MRS. SHIMERDA approaches the coffin with great reverence. SHE crosses herself then arranges the body—his arms and hands the way they should be. SHE takes an open prayer book from Ambroz and places it on the body. SHE makes the sign of the cross over the bandaged head. AMBROZ repeats her gesture as does ANNIE. MRS. SHIMERDA helps MAREK walk to the coffin and guides his hands in forming the blessing. SHE moves to YULKA who has been afraid to approach. The CHILD begins to cry wildly. MRS. SHIMERDA tries to guide the child's fingers but SHE screams. ANTONIA and TONY stop singing the lullaby.)*

GRANDMOTHER. *(Rushing to them.)* No, Mrs. Shimerda. I won't stand by and see that child frightened into spasms. She is too little to understand what you want of her. Let her alone.

*(MRS. SHIMERDA kneels holding Yulka in her arms. The other SHIMERDA CHILDREN press tightly around them. AMBROZ stands throughout upstage of his mother. OTTO and JAKE place the lid on the coffin, then firmly nail it down pounding with heavy hammers. The FAMILY reacts to the hammer blows as if they were gun shots.)*

MRS. SHIMERDA. Mr. Burden—please—to make—some prayers—here in English—for all.

(*EVERYONE except AMBROZ and GRANDFATHER kneel.*)

GRANDFATHER. (*Hands to heaven.*) Oh great and just God, no man among us knows what the sleeper knows, nor is it for us to judge what lies between him and Thee. If any man here has been remiss toward this stranger come to a far country, God will forgive him and soften his heart. Loving Father smooth the way before this widow and her children, and incline the hearts of men to deal justly with her. We leave Mr. Shimerda at Thy judgment seat, which is also Thy mercy seat.

ALL. Amen.

(*The MEN stand and uncoil the ropes. MAREK begins rocking back and forth like a wounded animal. GRANDMOTHER and JIMMY stand.*)

GRANDMOTHER. Can't you start a hymn, Otto? It would seem less heathenish.

(*OTTO begins singing "Jesus, Lover of My Soul." HE is joined by all the MEN as THEY lower the box into the frozen earth.*)

OTTO. Jesus, lover of my soul, let me to thy bosom fly, while the nearer waters roll, while the tempest still is high. Hide me, O my Savior, hide, till the storm of life is past, safe into the haven guide; O receive my soul at last.

*(The coffin has reached the bottom of the grave. MAREK stops rocking. JAKE, OTTO, KRAJIEK kneel at the open grave. GRANDFATHER embraces GRAND-MOTHER and JIMMY. MRS. SHIMERDA remains kneeling with MAREK and her DAUGHTERS. This funeral tableau holds in place as JIM BURDEN (no coat) enters stage left. ANTONIA enters with no coat from right carrying Papa's violin case in her arms. SHE touches her mother tenderly as if reaching back to a frozen memory.)*

JIM. Years afterward, when the open grazing days were over, and the roads no longer ran about like wild things, Mr. Shimerda's grave was still there, with a sagging wire fence around it, and an unpainted wooden cross. Never a tired driver passed the wooden cross, I am sure, without wishing well to the sleeper.

ANTONIA. After coming to America, Father never once played the violin he treasured so dearly and had played so merrily in the old country. However, on every brilliant, breathless summer day, as the breezes turn the golden wheatfields into rippling oceans, I hear my papa's music singing—singing.

**CURTAIN**

**END ACT I**

# ACT II
## Scene 1

### The Harlings

*Five years have passed. We are in Black Hawk, the
Harling's sitting room, just off the kitchen and the
porch. The room features an upright piano and informal
furniture. GRANDMOTHER, FRANCES and NINA
are awaiting Antonia's arrival.*

GRANDMOTHER. I thank God every day that if I have
to live in town, I live next door to the Harlings!
MRS. HARLING. Emmaline what a thing to say.
GRANDMOTHER. It's the truth, Mildred. Haven't we
put in our gardens together for three years now? Frances,
you and your father have been invaluable to Josiah in his
business transactions, Jimmy and Charley are almost
brothers and of course (*SHE opens her arms to NINA, who
runs to her.*) little Nina is my pet.

(*JAMES and CHARLEY bound in from the porch.*)

JAMES. They're here, Grandmother! They're here.
Excuse me, Mrs. Harling. Ambroz is just hitching up the
horses.
CHARLEY. Such a funny old-fashioned wagon.

77

MRS. HARLING. You be respectful, Charley Harling. You boys get right back out there and give him some help. Get some water and hay to his team.

GRANDMOTHER. Oh I do hope I've done the right thing. If only these years as a farm laborer haven't hardened her.

MRS. HARLING. I can bring something out of that girl. She's barely seventeen. Not too old to learn new ways.

FRANCES. I've been out to the Shimerda farm on business for father any number of times. I think the girl will be perfect. Mother cannot manage this house and family without domestic help and when that Danish girl left us we all thought your suggestion of Antonia exactly right. You see *we* are thankful the Burdens are just next door.

CHARLEY. Here they are! Here they are!

*(AMBROZ and TONY enter. THEY are dressed in simple but well-fitting farm clothes. SHE carries a small valise. THEY are followed by JAMES and CHARLEY.)*

GRANDMOTHER. Antonia!

TONY. Mrs. Burden!

GRANDMOTHER. (*Embracing Antonia.*) Hello my dear, how little and how much you have changed! You're so brown. Ambroz you've been working her too hard on the farm.

TONY. (*Overlapping, as THEY embrace.*) Thank you for remembering me, Mrs. Burden. We are to be neighbors again. From Mother I bring her kindest regards to you and to Mr. Burden.

GRANDMOTHER. God bless you, child, now you are come you must try to do right and be a credit to us. This is Antonia Shimerda and her brother Ambroz, my friend, Mrs. Harling.

MRS. HARLING. Do sit down. (*THEY don't.*) You boys are excused now.

CHARLEY. Oh Mama, really.

*(HE and JAMES stamp out.)*

GRANDMOTHER. Frances did I understand that you know each other?

TONY. Afternoon, Miss Frances. Thank you for asking me to come to town. I will do good work for you and Mrs. Harling. I am very strong and dear Mrs. Burden taught me so many things in her beautiful kitchen and I eager—I am eager to learn from you. Who is this little angel hiding away?

MRS. HARLING. Our youngest daughter Nina and the only shy Harling in Black Hawk.

TONY. (*Kneeling by Nina.*) My little sister was also very shy. Please be my friend. I don't know how to live in town, Nina. Will you help me?

*(NINA manages a nod.)*

AMBROZ. All wages will be paid to me. Three dollars every week. And you must buy shoes, give her bed and food.

MRS. HARLING. Now young man, your sister must have her own money here in town.

AMBROZ. Money is for family and farm place, not Antonia.

MRS. HARLING. She must have some money of her own.

AMBROZ. (*To Frances.*) Not what you say. (*AMBROZ puts on his hat and turns toward the door.*)

MRS. HARLING. We will pay the full wage as we offered—and a generous wage it is—but a girl cannot live in town with no spending money of her own.

AMBROZ. I must hire man to do work on the farm if she is here. Come Antonia.

FRANCES. There is no question of our paying full wages, but surely you understand she must have some personal money.

AMBROZ. Three dollars each week paid to me! (*AMBROZ pulls his hat on and off several times throughout this exchange.*)

FRANCES. That is impossible.

AMBROZ. We leave, Antonia.

GRANDMOTHER. (*Taking him by the shoulders and sitting him down.*) Listen to me Ambroz Shimerda. The Harlings are among the finest people in Black Hawk, Nebraska. They will care for your sister as if she were their own kin. A fair portion of her wages can go to your mother and you, but some small part must go to her.

TONY. No—I need no money—I come to town only to help my family. Money will pay mortgages and plows.

GRANDMOTHER. Don't be ridiculous. You must have spending money in town. We're all proud of your nice farmhouse and the way you have managed these years since your father's death. But things will be different for you here.

MRS. HARLING. I will retain one dollar each week for Antonia. Two dollars will go to the Shimerda farm.

AMBROZ. (*Rising.*) *And* shoes, *and* food, *and* bed.

FRANCES. Yes, yes of course. All of the hired girls in town have these arrangements.

TONY. (*Very embarrassed.*) Mother say she send three fat geese each year to make even for the shoes.

MRS. HARLING. (*Embracing her.*) How thoughtful my dear.

(*SALLY, 14, and HAROLD, 12, race into the room.*)

HAROLD. Mama, Sally won't stop pushing me.

MRS. HARLING. Here's the rest of the Harling tribe, Harold, my musician and naughty Sally, my tomboy.

FRANCES. Ambroz if you will come with me to Father's office I'll pay you for this first month in advance.

(*FRANCES and AMBROZ exit. JAMES quickly crosses DS. During the following narration HAROLD plays the PIANO. GRANDMOTHER will exit and the OTHERS will adjust for the following scene. ANTONIA adds an apron to her costume.*)

JAMES. How good it was to have Antonia near us again; to see her every day.

MRS. HARLING. Her greatest fault, was that she so often stopped her work and fell to playing with the children.

CHARLEY. She would race about the orchard with us, or take sides in our hay fights in the barn.

SALLY. Or be the old bear that came down from the mountain and carried off Nina.

MRS. HARLING. Everything she said seemed to come right out of her heart.

*(MRS. HARLING and CHARLEY are seated in the Harling's sitting room. TONY brings in freshly baked and frosted cupcakes. FRANCES follows with a stack of small plates, napkins and forks as JAMES, SALLY, HAROLD and NINA torment Tony with a song they have made up.)*

JAMES and the CHILDREN. I won't have none of your weevily wheat, and I won't have none of your barley, But I'll take a measure of fine white flour, to make a cake for Charley.

*(Suddenly LENA appears outside, on the porch.)*

LENA. Hello! Hello!

NINA. Look. Who's that?

LENA. *(Very well dressed with a hat, stockings and shoes.)* Hello Tony. Don't you know me?

TONY. Why, it's Lena! Of course I didn't know you, so dressed up!

LENA. Hello Jim. I've come to town to work too, Tony.

TONY. *(Still standing at the door.)* Have you now? Well, ain't that funny!

TINY. (*Almost popping out from behind Lena in her short skirt and striped stockings.*) Hey everybody, I'm Bridget Soderball, but my papa calls me Tiny. Oh my!

(*SHE and TONY hug each other.*)

FRANCES. Hello Tiny, I've done some business for your father and you are Lena Lengard, aren't you? I've been to see your mother, but you were off herding cattle that day. Mama, this is Chris Lengard's oldest girl. Please come in and join us.

(*ANTONIA starts for the kitchen.*)

FRANCES. Leave the kitchen for a while now, Antonia. Come visit with your company and serve all of us a slice of Charley's favorite cake.

MRS. HARLING. So you have come to town, where are you working?

LENA. For Mrs. Thomas, the dressmaker. She is going to teach me to sew. She says I have quite a knack. I'm through with the farm. There ain't any end to the work on a farm, and always so much trouble happens.

TINY. I've got a place with Mrs. Gardner at the Boys Home Hotel. My mama says she started behind in farm work and never caught up. Now I can help with extra money. Besides, at the hotel I'll meet lots of strangers. The Marshall Field man come in today and that Willie O'Riley, the furniture salesman from Kansas City, has been with us all week. (*Up on her tiptoes.*) Oh my!

MRS. HARLING. I don't think a hotel's a good place for a girl, so you take care, Tiny.

TINY. Yes ma'am, I will.

LENA. We only come to town so as to help our folks. We can send them money.

MRS. HARLING. See that you don't forget to. And I wouldn't run down the farm —I grew up on a farm back in Ohio and I'm proud of it. So Mrs. Thomas thinks you can be a dressmaker?

LENA. Yes, 'm. I've always liked to sew, but I never had much to do with. Mrs. Thomas makes lovely things for all the town ladies. Did you know Mrs. Gardener is having a purple velvet made? The velvet came from Omaha. My but it's lovely.

TINY. (*Finishing the last crumb of her cake*.) Come on Lena, oh my, Samson d'Arnault's playing for a sing-along at the Hotel tonight. If we don't scurry we'll miss it. (*SHE heads to the door*.)

FRANCES. Please stop by again, any time you feel lonesome or need advice about anything.

LENA. Thank you, m'am, but I don't see how anybody could be lonesome in town. (*SHE pulls ANTONIA to the porch*.) Please come see me, Tony. I've got a room of my own at Mrs. Thomas'. Please come see me.

TINY. And the traveling men at the hotel is such gentlemen. Oh my!

TONY. Sometimes Lena, Tiny, but Mrs. Harling don't like to have me run out much.

LENA. You can do what you please when you go out. Ain't you crazy about town, Tony? I don't care what anybody says, I'm done with the farm.

TINY. Me too!

(*THEY exit, ANTONIA re-enters the sitting room.*)

FRANCES. Why weren't you a little more cordial, Antonia?

TONY. I didn't know if your mother would like them coming here. They was kind of talked about out in the country as being fast.

*(SHE and FRANCES share a naughty laugh.*
*During the following narration, the HARLINGS move a table to the center of the room. HAROLD once again plays his recital piece at the piano under MRS. HARLING's close supervision. ANTONIA enters from the kitchen with a bowl of nuts.)*

JAMES. Winter comes down savagely over a little town on the prairie. The wind that sweeps in from the open country strips away all the leafy screens that hide one yard from another in summer, and the houses seem to draw closer together. *(JAMES joins the Harlings.)*

TONY. *(Pouring the nuts out on the table.)* We must separate all of the hulls from the kernels if we want walnut taffy. *(The hulls are tossed into a bowl.)*

NINA. Tell us a story, please Tony.

SALLY. We won't work without a good story!

HAROLD. Yes Tony, please.

TONY. I can't think of a story tonight.

CHARLEY. Please, Antonia we need a good story.

TONY. You know Mrs. Harling, how we've all heard that the Spanish army came up into this country long years ago with that Coronado searching for the Seven Golden Cities?

HAROLD. Them's just tales, my teacher at school told us they never ever got so far north as Nebraska.

TONY. (*With elaborate exaggeration SHE acts out the story.*) Well, last summer when I was threshing up in the Norwegian settlement, Ole Iverson was breaking sod and turned up a silver stirrup of fine workmanship and a big sword with a Spanish inscription on the blade. Father Kelly found the name of the Spanish maker on the sword and three letters that stood for the city of Cordova over there in Spain. And, I saw them with my own eyes. Now don't that prove the teacher was wrong and those tales are true?

CHARLEY. (*Taking the imaginary sword from Tony.*) I'll just bet you old Coronado used that sword to chop off the heads of every little girl he could find up here.

(*HE pretends to chop off Nina's head. SHE begins to wail.*)

TONY. Charley you've got Nina all upset. Don't you cry, no Spanish cutthroat will get you while Tony's here.

MRS. HARLING. Stop crying, Nina, or I'll always send you upstairs when Antonia tells us stories. Isn't that taffy nearly ready to eat? I've been smelling it a long while.

(*TONY races for the kitchen and re-enters with a cooking pan of hot taffy. FRANCES follows her, re-entering with a bowl of butter. The kernels are spread on the table and the taffy is placed in four mounds on top.*)

FRANCES. Butter your fingers everyone, so you won't get burned. Jimmy are you pulling with me?

*(EVERYONE shouts as THEY team up for taffy pulling. ANTONIA sings her childhood Bohemian song, soon THEY are all singing with her at the top of their lungs. MR. HARLING enters suddenly ducking under ropes of taffy.)*

MR. HARLING. What in thundering tarnation is going on here? Mildred, you can be heard blocks away! This is my home, not a carnival and all of you know that.

MRS. HARLING. I'm sorry, Jasper, quite sorry. I don't know what came over me. Take this to the kitchen, children, quietly. Say "Welcome home" to your father.

*(The CHILDREN meekly remove the table and murmur greetings to Mr. Harling.)*

FRANCES. It's fresh walnut taffy, Papa. I know it's your favorite. I'll bring some to your room after while. *(FRANCES exits, following the others to the kitchen.)*

MR. HARLING. It's that Bohemian girl, Mildred. She's a bad influence here.

MRS. HARLING. No Jasper, the children love her and her work is superb.

MR. HARLING. Are you quarreling with me, Mildred?

MRS. HARLING. Oh forgive me dear, if it seemed so. I'll make you some fresh coffee and bring it right up to your desk. Won't that be nice?

*(MRS. CUTTER, a large, very excitable woman appears on the porch. SHE carries a basket of her hand-painted china.)*

MRS. CUTTER. (*Bellowing*.) Save me, Mildred. Help me! Mr. Cutter has turned me out, forced me from my family home. He has cursed my dear parents and all of my people. He thinks I'm trying to steal his ill-gotten money. That's not true! You know better, everyone in town knows better.

(*MRS. HARLING tries to quiet her and assist her to a chair. JAMES, ANTONIA and the HARLING CHILDREN peer in from the kitchen.*)

MRS. CUTTER. Why did God smite me with such an evil, evil man? I've always been a Christian and my folk are the finest family—you know that!

(*WICK CUTTER, a thin man with a full yellow beard, rages in from the porch.*)

MR. CUTTER. You've disgraced yourself this time, Mrs. Cutter. A public spectacle you are, you fat old cow!

MR. HARLING. Wick Cutter out of my house. My beloved little ones are here.

MR. CUTTER. We'd have little ones too, if Mrs. Cutter had not purposely remained childless. She's determined to outlive me, to share my hard-earned fortune with her detestable people.

MR. HARLING. (*Trying to remove Cutter forcibly from the room.*) Not another word. This vile behavior will not happen in my sitting room.

MRS. CUTTER. Didn't you order me out of the home left me by my sainted father?

MR and MRS. HARLING. Stop—No more—silence!—This won't do.

MR. CUTTER. I held the mortgage on the miserable house, as I do on most every house in the county.

MRS. CUTTER. If I must wander the streets earning my own pitiful sustenance, praise be God, I'm an artist! (*SHE holds up one of her hideous painted plates.*) I am now compelled to live by my brush.

MR. CUTTER. You've disfigured a million dishes with your paint. I've had enough of it!

(*MR. CUTTER lunges past Mr. Harling and grabs up one of the small pained bowls in her basket, as the HARLINGS try to stop him.*)

MRS. CUTTER. (*Very loud and very grand.*) Mr. Cutter, you have broken all the Commandments—spare the finger bowls!

(*MR. CUTTER stops before smashing the bowl to the floor. HE begins laughing. MRS. CUTTER laughs with him, THEY roar with laughter as the OTHERS stare at them amazed.*)

MR. CUTTER. (*Offering his arm with a polite little bow.*) Shall we be off to home now, Mrs. Cutter?

MRS. CUTTER. (*Taking his arm lovingly.*) Thank you, Mr. Cutter.

MR. CUTTER. May I carry this heavy basket for you, dear?

MRS. CUTTER. Why yes, Mr. Cutter.

MR. CUTTER. (*Brushing past Mr. Harling.*) Thank you for your gracious hospitality. Good evening.

MR. HARLING. Mildred, the Cutters are not welcome in my house. We must shield the children.

MRS. HARLING. Yes dear. I'm so sorry. It will never happen again.

(*The Harling set pivots offstage.*)

## ACT II
### Scene 2

### The Dancing Pavilion

JAMES. Mrs. Harling deferred to Mr. Harling in everything. Fortunately for us children, his business kept him away for weeks at a time. When boys and girls are growing up, life can't stand still, not even in the smallest of country towns; and they have to grow up, whether they will or no. That is what their elders are always forgetting.

TONY. The summer which was to change everything was coming nearer every day.

(*LENA and TINY race on.*)

LENA. Have you seen it?

TINY. The new dancing pavilion, Oh my!

LENA. On the vacant lot next to the Danish laundry. It looks like a merry-go-round back home in Oslo.

TINY. Dances every night, but Sunday. At last something to do after work. All the men will be there. The Marshall Field's man, Oh my! has already asked me for the first dance. I said yes. Oh, oh, oh!

*(The canopy of LIGHTS that form the Dancing Pavilion lower into place.)*

LENA. Jimmy, you're dancing with me. Come on Tony.
TONY. But Mrs. Harling won't like it.

*(SHE runs with them. The pavilion LIGHTS up, the MUSIC blasts out, the DANCERS are whirling. There are very few women.)*

HARRY. You're the Harling's hired girl, ain't ya? You're even prettier than folks been saying. What's ya name?
TONY. *(Softly.)* Tony.
HARRY. Well, Mrs. Harling's Tony, let's dance.

*(SHE is swept away. Tony is obviously the belle of the ball. As the dance continues, MRS. HARLING enters.)*

MRS. HARLING. From then on Antonia hummed dance tunes all day. When supper was late, she hurried with her dishes, dropped and smashed them in her excitement. At the first call of the music, she became irresponsible.

*(The MUSIC, with it's call of remembered youth, sweeps MRS. HARLING into it's spell. SHE dances alone and*

*unobserved by the farmers, traveling men and hired girls under the canopy of twinkling lights. FRANCES enters, also bewitched by the music.)*

FRANCES. Antonia's success at the tent had its consequences. The iceman lingered too long now. Young farmers who were in town for Saturday came tramping to the back yard to engage dances. (*The music changes to "Home Sweet, Home."*) The boys who brought her home after the dances sometimes laughed at the back gate and wakened Papa from his first sleep.

MRS. HARLING. A crisis was inevitable.

*(MRS. HARLING and FRANCES exit as the DANCERS start for home.)*

HARRY. Come on, Tony, let me walk you home tonight. It's my turn.

LENA. Ain't you something, Harry Paine, Tony knows you're marrying your boss' daughter on Monday?

HARRY. Come on Tony, that don't make no never mind. Please just let me see you safely home so that none of these rascals give you any trouble.

TINY. You'll be a married man by Monday night—My, oh, my.

HARRY. Monday is Monday and this is Saturday. Come on Tony, we've been dancing all night, I don't see no difference.

LENA. (*Grabbing James' arm.*) Come on Mr. Burden, I need some masculine protection, too.

TINY. My-my-my. (*SHE grabs the Marshall Field's man and THEY are quickly off.*)

TONY. You may not hold my hand.

HARRY Of course not, we'll just talk a bit as we walk.

*(TONY and HARRY begin their stroll home.)*

TONY. Harry, I'm wishing you every happiness in your married life.

HARRY. *(As THEY near the Harling gate.)* That's nice, Tony. You can start things off right by helping me tonight.

TONY. How's that Harry?

HARRY. You see, I'm mighty tense just waiting and you country girls know all the tricks.

*(HE grabs for her arms and holds her tight in a kiss. SHE struggles and at last frees an arm and slaps him hard across the face. HARRY runs away. MR. HARLING enters quickly.)*

MR. HARLING. This is what I've been expecting, Antonia. You've been going out with girls who have a reputation for being free and easy. Now people think the same of you. I won't have it! This is the end of it, tonight. It stops short. You can quit going to these dances, or you can hunt another place!

TONY. Stop going to the dances? I wouldn't think of it for a minute.

*(SHE runs inside. MR. HARLING follows her. Far upstage, in the glow of the pavilion lights, COUPLES continue dancing.)*

JAMES. (*Sitting alone on the floor DS.*) One dream I dreamed a great many times was always the same. I was in a harvest field full of shocks, and I was lying against one of them. Lena Lengard came across the stubble barefoot, in a short skirt. She was flushed like the dawn, with a kind of luminous rosiness all about her. She sat down beside me, turned to me with a soft sigh and said, "Now they are all gone, and I can kiss you as much as I like." I used to wish I could have this flattering dream about Antonia, but I never did.

(*The Harling's sitting room. MRS. HARLING and FRANCES are waiting. TONY enters with her valise. The dance continues upstage.*)

TONY. Mr. Harling ain't my boss outside my work. I won't give up my friends or stop going to the dances neither. I thought Mr. Paine was nice because he used to come here. I guess I gave him a red face for his wedding, alright.

MRS. HARLING. I can't go back on what Mr. Harling has said. This is his house.

TONY. Then I'll just leave. The Cutters want me to come to them. They pay four dollars there and the work's nothing.

FRANCES. Antonia, if you go to work for the Cutters you cannot come back to this house again.

MRS. HARLING. You know what that man is.

TONY. I can take care of myself. I'm a lot stronger than Cutter is. Don't I deserve a good time like the other girls? (*SHE is near tears, picks up her valise and rushes from the room.*)

MRS. HARLING. I wish I had never let myself become fond of her.

*(The sitting room moves off. The pavilion LIGHTS are suddenly snapped off. The DANCERS disperse. JAMES stands, JIM BURDEN brings James a collar, tie and coat. During the following narration JIM assists JAMES in dressing. The pavilion lights fly up out of sight.)*

## ACT II
## Scene 3

### Fireman's Hall

JIM. The dancing pavilion was taken down once September came, but after Antonia went to live with the Cutters. She seemed to care about nothing but parties and the notorious Saturday night dances at Fireman's hall.

*(The adult ANTONIA—approx. age 22—now in feathers and one of Lena Lengard's high fashion gowns enters abruptly pulling on her long gloves as SHE cuts between James and Jim. The garish decorations for the Fireman's hall lower into place. The dancing resumes with a flourish. The FARMERS have added collars, ties and jackets. The HIRED GIRLS shine in their feathers and daring bare-shouldered dresses. Dancing resumes with a rougher feeling. The adult ANTONIA is now the center of attention.)*

JAMES. Antonia loved the catcalls and admiring glances she earned from every man in Black Hawk as she strutted down the street in the stylish dresses Lena Lengard created for her.

JIM. Tony wore gloves now, and high-heeled shoes with feathered bonnets. She was no longer a girl, she was a striking young woman. (*HE exits.*)

JAMES. (*Now dressed in a collar and coat.*) Like Antonia, dances at the Firemen's Hall became my favorite diversion. My grandparents would have been scandalized, so I waited until all was quiet and the old people were asleep, then raised my window and climbed out. The first time I deceived my grandparents I felt rather shabby, perhaps even the second time, but I soon ceased to think about it.

(*The dancing at the Fireman's Hall is far more rowdy than the restrained dances of the Pavilion. JAMES races up to join them and cuts in on Antonia. The band begins "Home, Sweet, Home." The COUPLES start for home, into the dark night.*)

TINY. (*A squeal as if someone had pinched her.*) Oh my—Oh—Oh my.

(*JAMES and ANTONIA begin strolling toward the Cutters.*)

JAMES. Tony's favorite partner was Larry Donovan, a railway conductor. But he was often away on his Burlington run to Denver. Now Tony, since I walked you home, you must let me kiss you. (*HE kisses her quickly.*)

ANTONIA. Jimmy, you know that ain't right. I'll tell your Grandmother on you.

JAMES. Lena Lengard lets me kiss her and I'm not half as fond of her as I am of you.

ANTONIA. She does? I'll scratch her eyes out.

JAMES. (*Kneeling and embracing her passionately.*) Oh Antonia, don't you know I care about you more than anyone else in the world? I would like to have you for a sweetheart, or wife, or mother, or sister anything a woman can be to a man. The idea of you is part of my mind; you influence my likes and dislikes when I don't even realize it. You really are a part of me.

ANTONIA. (*Kneeling as if to a child.*) Don't you go and be a fool like some of these town boys. You're not going to sit around here and whittle store boxes and tell stories all your life. You are going away to school and make something of yourself. I'm just awful proud of you. You won't go and get mixed up with the Swedes, will you?

JAMES. I don't care about any of them but you. And you'll always treat me like a kid, I suppose.

ANTONIA. (*Hugging him.*) I expect I will, but you're a kid I'm awful fond of.

(*THEY stand. SHE kisses him unexpectedly. THEY quickly exit.*)

## ACT II
### Scene 4

## Problems with Mr. Cutter

*Set shifts to the sitting room of the Burden home in Black Hawk. JAMES moves to GRANDMOTHER, who seems very upset and fretful.*

JAMES. What are you fretting about, Grandmother? Has Grandfather lost any money?

GRANDMOTHER. No, it ain't money. I wish it was. But I've heard things. You must'a known it would come back to me sometime. I was never one that claimed old folks could bring up their grandchildren. But it came about so; there wasn't any other way for you, it seemed like.

JAMES. What is it Grandmother? Is it the Firemen's dances? (*GRANDMOTHER nods.*) I'm sorry I sneaked off like that. But there's nothing wrong about the dances. I like all those country girls, Lena and Tiny, and I like to dance with them.

GRANDMOTHER. But it ain't right to deceive us, son, and it brings blame on us. People say you are growing up to be bad.

JAMES. I don't care what they say about me, but if it hurts you, that settles it. (*HE kisses her.*) I won't go to the Firemen's Hall again. (*Crossing DS, removing his coat collar and tie.*) I kept my promise, using most of those dull nights to write my Commencement Oration.

(*ANTONIA enters quickly, joining GRANDMOTHER and JAMES.*)

ANTONIA. Forgive me barging in, Mrs. Burden.

GRANDMOTHER. What is it child?

ANTONIA. It's Mr. Cutter, m'am. I'm frightened he means to scare me or something. You know Mrs. Cutter never stirs from Black Hawk without him. They've gone up to Lincoln to attend the funeral of Mrs. Cutter's Aunt Rebha. He said it was one less of her people after his money. (*THEY all laugh.*) Before he left he secretly put a new Yale lock on the door and put all of the silver in a box with his papers and pushed it under my bed. He forbade me allowing anyone in the house or having any of the girls stay with me at night. He made me promise to be home early each night and not stay out late for a party. He kept coming into the kitchen when Mrs. Cutter was packing her things upstairs to instruct me and I don't feel right about it.

GRANDMOTHER. I don't think it's right for you to stay there, but it wouldn't be right to leave the place unattended either. Maybe Jim would be willing to go over there and sleep. I'd feel safer knowing you were under my own roof.

ANTONIA. Would you Jim? I'll make up my bed nice and fresh for you. The bed is right by the window so the room stays nice and cool.

(*Antonia's room at the Cutters' has appeared. It is a simple maid's room with a small bed placed DS and parallel with the front of the stage. JAMES moves to it, speaking as HE undresses, turns back the bed covers, sleeping in his undershirt and shorts. GRAND-MOTHER and ANTONIA pivot off on the Burden set.*)

JAMES. I liked my own room, and I didn't like the Cutters' house under any circumstances, but Tony looked so troubled that I consented to try this arrangement. I found that I slept there as well as anywhere, and when I got home in the morning, Tony had a good breakfast waiting for me. After prayers she sat down at the table with us, and it was like old times in the country. (*Turning back the bed covers and lying down.*) The third night I spent at the Cutters' I awoke suddenly with the impression that I had heard a door open and shut. I must have gone to sleep again immediately.

(*MR. CUTTER enters the dark room. HE removes his coat, tie and shoes. HE lifts the covers and slips into bed. After a moment or two HE leans across the sleeping body, which HE assumes to be Antonia, and reaches to kiss her. HE strokes her cheek with his beard and purrs.*)

MR. CUTTER. Tony, Tony, your Wycliffe is here for his pretty girl.

(*JAMES awakes with a shout. MR. CUTTER holds him violently, then begins beating him.*)

MR. CUTTER. What in hell? So this is what she's doing while I'm away! Where is she? Where is the little slut? Under the bed are you hussy? I'll fix this rat you've got in your bed. He's caught, he's caught!

*(JAMES sends CUTTER sprawling on the floor. JAMES bounds out the window.)*

MR. CUTTER. Scoundrel! Break into my house will you? My notes—money—silver— *(HE drags the box from under the bed, almost sobbing as HE embraces the box.)* safe, all safe. I'll teach you to try robbing Wick Cutter.

*(The setting shifts back to the Burden's.)*

JAMES. Suddenly I found myself limping across the north end of Black Hawk in my nightshirt, just as one sometimes finds oneself behaving in bad dreams.

*(HE stumbles into the Burden home. GRANDFATHER enters with a lamp.)*

GRANDFATHER. Son, you startled us. Jim you're bleeding.

*(HE takes the boy into his arms. GRANDMOTHER and ANTONIA run on, crying out.)*

GRANDFATHER. I shall go immediately for the doctor.
JAMES. No. Find the sheriff. Cutter came home, he meant to ruin Tony. Thank God I was there instead.

*(MRS. CUTTER enters hysterically, followed by OTTO and JAKE. JAMES exits with ANTONIA.)*

MRS. CUTTER. Emmaline, my key no longer fits my own front door. What am I to do? I'm a homeless defenseless woman, unprotected in this cruel world. Mr. Cutter seated me so sweetly on the wrong train in Lincoln, and I've not seen him since. The devil! I hired a livery in Hastings and raced for Black Hawk, to find my house barred against me. Yours was the only light.

GRANDFATHER. Mr. Cutter is inside your home. He has wickedly attempted to murder our son.

MRS. CUTTER. We have the weasel trapped. Come gentlemen, we'll crash through the door! *(SHE marches them off.)*

## ACT II
### Scene 5

### The Commencement

*The ORGAN blares the introduction to the hymn "A Mighty Fortress." The CAST fills the stage for commencement. THEY are standing in "Sunday clothes," grouped as families facing the audience—MR. & MRS. BURDEN, JAKE & OTTO, the HARLINGS, ANTONIA, her MOTHER and BROTHER, and MR. & MRS. CUTTER. LENA and TINY stand with the MARSHALL FIELD'S MAN and WILLIE O'RILEY. THEY sing: "A mighty fortress is our God, A bulwark never failing." JAMES enters DS as if he had been speaking to the assembled cast.*

JAMES. Our commencement exercises were held in the Opera House. I thought my oration very good.

*(The CROWD surges toward James. GRANDMOTHER and GRANDFATHER reach him first. GRAND- FATHER shakes his hand vigorously as the OTHERS begin to speak.)*

GRANDMOTHER. Oh son, I've never been so proud!

JAKE. You didn't get that speech out of no book.

TINY. It must make you very happy to have fine thoughts like that. Oh my!

OTTO. As your Grandma would say, "you did us a real credit."

FRANCES. He won't tell you, of course, but your Grandfather was pleased. You surprised me, Jim. I didn't believe you could do that well.

CHARLEY. Good work, you son of a gun.

MRS. HARLING. I just can't stop crying. Now you're off to Lincoln and Charley to the Navy.

TINY. My oh my. Me and Lena are off too for San Francisco. Mrs. Gardener got me a place in a nice hotel and Lena will be dressmaking on her own out there. We'll be rich!

MRS. CUTTER. James Burden, you are the very image of my darling nephew Rufus and he'll being going to college too, just as soon as I come into a little money.

MR. CUTTER. *(Offhandedly to James.)* Good talk. *(To Mrs. Cutter.)* You ain't ever coming into my money to waste on that mangy family of yours!

MRS. CUTTER. *(Very sweetly.)* Now Mr. Cutter, it could be sooner than you think. *(Suddenly.)* You licentious son of Satan! (*SHE storms off without looking back to him.*) Sooner than you think! All mine!

MR. CUTTER. The sky over Jerusalem will be thick with pigs when that day comes. (*HE runs after her.*)

MRS. SHIMERDA. Good speech. Much good speech. I always want my children to go to school.

ANTONIA. Jim, it was splendid!

LENA. What made you so solemn? I thought you were scared.

(*As the CROWD thins out.*)

ANTONIA. I just sat there wishing my papa could hear you, Jim. There was something in your speech that made me think of my papa.

JAMES. I thought about your papa when I wrote my speech, Tony. His dignity. I dedicated it to him.

LENA. So now you're off to the University and Law School at Harvard?

JAMES. I must excel in Lincoln, before they will accept me at Harvard.

ANTONIA, TINY & LENA. You will Jim—We know it—Oh my!

JAMES. Antonia, you helped me know what I really want to do with my life. My mind's made up.

LENA. All your Burdens are so hardheaded! You should leave room for a bit of fun now and then!

(*TINY and LENA exit with their MEN friends, ANTONIA embraces James.*)

ANTONIA. This means you are going from us for good, and that's right. But it don't mean I'll lose you. My papa's been dead all these years and yet he's more real to me than ever. The older I grow the more I understand him.

*(THEY exit together.)*

## ACT II
## Scene 6

### Leaving for Denver

*JIM BURDEN and JIMMY enter. During the following narration the scene shifts back to the Burden home. A sewing machine has been added.*

JIM. The following summer Antonia announced her intention to marry Larry Donovan. Larry Donovan was a passenger conductor, what you might call a train crew aristocrat, afraid someone might ask him to put up a pullman car window.

JIMMY. If requested to perform such a menial service Donovan would silently point to the button that calls the porter, then leisurely continue his stroll through the train car.

JIM. He was a self-appointed ladies man. With men he was cold and distant but with women he had a grave familiarity and he was always able to make some foolish heart ache. Antonia fell for him.

*(ANTONIA is singing a Bohemian song as SHE works at the sewing machine. JIM scoops JIMMY onto his shoulders and jogs off as GRANDMOTHER enters.)*

GRANDMOTHER. Antonia, don't run that machine so fast. You won't hasten the day none that way.

MRS. HARLING. *(Entering.)* I hear you're off for Denver, Tony. I'm disappointed. We all wanted to toss rice at your wedding. You are certainly pretty enough for any man.

ANTONIA. Denver frightens me, but his letter said he's in line for a big promotion, and we'll be married there. I'm a country girl, I doubt if I'll be able to manage for him in a city. I was counting on keeping chickens and maybe a cow.

AMBROZ. *(Enters with a velvet covered box.)* Mother wanted you to have this, it's a set of plated table silver.

MRS. HARLING. Now that'll be just fine in Denver, Tony.

AMBROZ. *(HE pulls his sister privately to one side.)* This is for you. *(HE takes out an envelope)* I figured your wages for these years you worked out, Antonia. It's near three hundred dollars. Papa would have wanted you to have it as you start out.

*(ANTONIA and AMBROZ embrace.)*

MRS. HARLING. You're behaving like a man, Ambroz and I'm glad to see it.

*(ANTONIA returns to her sewing machine with GRANDMOTHER and MRS. HARLING as the set moves off.)*

## ACT II
### Scene 7

### The Cutter Murder

*Two GUNSHOT BLASTS—spaced separately are heard offstage. The Cutter maid's room appears. MR. CUTTER lies on the bed, embracing his strongbox. HIS throat is torn open. HE is bleeding onto a roll of sheets and pillows HE has placed beside his head. As HE appears HE fires a third shot through the window. The MEN call from offstage, overlapping.*

| GRAND-FATHER. | JAKE. | HARRY. | OTTO. | HARLING. |
|---|---|---|---|---|
| Cutter, are you alright? | Land sakes! | Cutter, what's going on? | You need help in there? | Thundering tarnation! |

GRANDFATHER. (*After a pause.*) We're coming in there Cutter.

*(The horrified MEN stumble into the room.)*

CUTTER. (*Weakly.*) Walk in, gentlemen, I'm alive, you see, and competent. You are witnesses that I have survived my wife. You will find her in her own room. Please make your examination at once, so there will be no mistake.

*(JAKE, HARLING and HARRY rush out to the next room. GRANDFATHER and OTTO kneel to assist CUTTER.)*

OTTO. I'll step to the parlor and telephone the doctor.

GRANDFATHER. Did you inflict this wound on yourself?

*(THEY re-enter one by one.)*

JAKE. She's in there, Mr. Burden, lying on the bed in her nightgown and wrapper. Looks like she's taking a nap. Only thing is—ya' see—she's shot through the heart.

HARRY. Must 'a been a close shot. I'm tellin' you there's powder burns on her wrapper.

MR. CUTTER. Mrs. Cutter is quite dead, gentlemen. I am conscious. My affairs are in order.

*(MR. HARLING enters.)*

GRANDFATHER. *(Reverently.)* Dear God in heaven, *(Pause.)* he's dead.

OTTO. *(Re-entering.)* Doctor will be right over.

JAKE. Ain't no need, theys both gone already!

MR. HARLING. Look at this letter, he's dated it for five o'clock this afternoon. *(Skimming the letter quickly.)* He has shot his wife—any will she might have secretly made is invalid as he survived her—he means to shoot himself at six o'clock—and will—strength permitting—fire a shot through the window—in hopes that neighbors or passers-by might come in and see him—before life was extinct.

GRANDFATHER. Would you have thought even Cutter to be cruel enough for such a stunt? To do that woman out of any comfort she might have from his money after he was gone? Who's left to benefit?

OTTO. Did you ever hear tell of anybody that killed himself for spite? (*The MEN begin to laugh.*) Pure old spite!

GRANDFATHER. (*Laughing with the others.*) He scraped together a fortune by ruthless means only to die for it in the end. (*THEY laugh.*)

(*The set moves off, leaving only the Nebraska sky. GRANDMOTHER enters in an apron and sunbonnet.*)

## ACT II
## Scene 8

### The Shimerda's Field

GRANDMOTHER. We received a postcard saying Antonia had arrived in Denver and they were to be married in a few days, then no further word. Nearly a year later Otto reported he had seen a woman plowing in the Shimerda's field. She was so bundled he couldn't tell for sure but he thought it must be Antonia. (*GRANDMOTHER crosses US, waves her apron and calls.*) Leave your work Antonia, I must see you. We met like the people in the old song, in silence if not in tears.

*(ANTONIA enters in the family overcoat which is much too large for her. SHE is pregnant. GRANDMOTHER tries to embrace her.)*

ANTONIA. You'll make me cry and I don't want to. *(Moving DS.)* I'm not married and I ought to be.

GRANDMOTHER. Oh my child, what's happened?

ANTONIA. He's run away from me, I don't know if he ever meant to marry me.

GRANDMOTHER. You mean he's thrown up his job and quit the country?

ANTONIA. He didn't have any job. He'd been fired; blacklisted for knocking down fares. I didn't know. I thought he hadn't been treated right. He lived with me till my money ran out, and then he just didn't come back. One nice fellow at the station told me, when I kept going to look for him, to give it up. He said he was afraid Larry'd gone bad and wouldn't come back any more. I guess he's gone to Old Mexico. The conductors get rich down there, collecting half-fares off the natives and robbing the company.

GRANDMOTHER. Why didn't you insist on a civil marriage?

ANTONIA. I guess my patience was wore out, waiting so long. I thought if he saw how well I could do for him, he'd want to stay with me.

*(The WOMEN embrace. GRANDMOTHER kneels sobbing into her apron. ANTONIA gently slips away. During the following speech the SKY changes to an ominous winter mood.)*

GRANDMOTHER. Antonia worked on through the harvest and threshing. On a snowy December evening after getting her cattle in, Antonia went to her room and shut the door. There, without calling to anybody, without a groan, she lay down and bore her child.

*(Offstage the ANTONIAS are singing the Bohemian lullaby. The lullaby continues as MRS. SHIMERDA rushes toward Grandmother holding the new-born baby in her arms. AMBROZ is chasing her.)*

MRS. SHIMERDA. *(Shrieking—partly in Czech.)* No—stop it—nyet—nyet—Ambroz—monster—monster—nyet—nyet! Never!

AMBROZ. Throw it in the rain barrel. Bastard in the rain barrel. Shame on us, disgrace. Neighbors laugh, say illegitimate bastard. Put it in the rain barrel. *(HE reaches for the baby.)*

GRANDMOTHER. There's a law in this land, don't you forget that. Your mother and I stand as witness that this baby has come into the world sound and strong and I intend to keep an eye on what befalls her.

*(GRANDMOTHER holds MRS. SHIMERDA in her arms. THEY take the baby to safety. AMBROZ follows them in disgust. The lullaby has ended. The LIGHTS change as JAMES and JIMMY run into the same field at sunset in early spring.)*

JAMES. A few months later, before I left for Boston, I returned briefly to Black Hawk. Everyone was saying you know about poor Antonia? Poor Antonia. I drove out to the farm. Whatever disappointment she felt in herself, she felt only pride for her child.

JIMMY. (*Waving happily.*) Antonia came running towards me as if we were still children, with her baby in her arms.

(*TONY and ANNIE race to them. ANNIE carries the baby, now four months old. ANNIE and JIMMY kneel, rocking the baby together.*)

ANNIE. Ain't she pretty, Jimmy? Did you ever in your life see anything pretty as my Martha?

JAMES. She looks just like you.

TONY. You're off for Law School? There ain't a lawyer in Black Hawk can speak as well as you. I can't wait till my little girl's old enough to tell her about the things we used to do.

ANNIE. You'll always remember me when you think about old times, won't you?

TONY. I guess everybody thinks about old times, even the happiest of people. As we walked homeward across the field, the sun dropped and lay like a great golden globe in the west.

ANNIE. While it hung there, the moon rose in the east as big as a cart-wheel, pale silver and streaked with rose color.

JAMES. For five, perhaps ten minutes, the two luminaries confronted each other across the level land, resting on opposite edges of the world. I felt the old pull of the earth, the solemn magic that comes out of those fields at nightfall.

JIMMY. I wished I could be a little boy again and my way could end there.

JAMES. I had to look hard to see her face, which I meant to always carry with me, at the very bottom of my memory.

JIMMY and JAMES. I'll come back!

TONY. Perhaps you will. (*SHE smiles.*)

ANNIE. But even if you don't, you're here like my father. So I won't be lonesome.

(*THEY embrace then depart reluctantly, exiting separate ways, the ANTONIAS into the moonlight and the JIM BURDENS into the fading sunset.*)

JAMES. Grandmother wrote me joyfully two years later of Antonia's marriage to Anton Cuzak, a Bohemian farmer whom Grandmother admired. (*HE is quickly off.*)

## ACT II
## Scene 9

### Antonia's Legacy

*The CHILDREN are singing Annie's happy Bohemian song in the fruit cave as the doors are pushed open. JIM BURDEN and ANTONIA climb up arm in arm.*

ANTONIA. Come look Jim, if the corn isn't too tall we can see the very top of your Grandfather's old windmill. Of course our old farm lies just beyond. Think how proud my papa must be to see the way Ambroz has made the old place pay off. I do hope they will come over while you are here. Ambroz's wife suits him perfectly. A stout German woman. (*Wickedly—but unable to resist the temptation—SHE puffs her cheeks.*) Fat—like—butter!

(*THEY laugh.*)

JIM. How like you, Antonia, to see the joy in things everyone else thinks of as commonplace.

ANTONIA. I love her so! She bosses dear Ambroz just the way Mama always did.

JIM. Antonia, no matter whatever we may have missed, we share our memories of the past.

ANTONIA. Have you learned to like big cities, Jim?

JIM. Yes, in many ways I have.

ANTONIA. (*As the CHILDREN stop singing.*) I'd always be miserable in a city. I'd die of lonesomeness. I like to be where I know every stack and tree, and where all the ground is friendly. It was a pretty hard job, breaking up this place and making the first crops grow! My babies came along so fast, but we all just kept on working and I'm so glad. I want to live and die here. Father Kelly says everybody's put into this world for something, and I know my purpose now.

JIM. You ought never to have gone to town, Tony.

ANTONIA. Oh, I'm glad I went! I learned nice ways at the Harlings', and I've been able to bring my children up so much better. Don't you think they are pretty well-behaved for country children? If it hadn't been for what Mrs. Harling taught me, I expect I'd have brought them up like wild rabbits. No, I'm glad I had a chance to learn; but

I'm thankful none of my daughters will ever have to hire out. (*SHE moves to the fruit cave door calling.*) Children! Children! The trouble with me, Jim, is I never could believe harm of anybody I loved.

JIM. We turned to leave the cave; Antonia and I went up the stairs first, and the children waited. We were standing outside talking, when they all came running up the steps together, big and little, tow heads and gold heads and brown, and flashing little naked legs; a veritable explosion of life out of the dark cave into the sunlight. It made me dizzy for a moment. Antonia was a rich mine of life, like the founder of early races.

(*During the narration, the CHILDREN have exploded from the cave. The CHILDREN tumble around their mother and Jim. ANTON and LEO close the cave doors. JIM steps over to assist.*)

LEO. We're mighty pleased you've come out to visit Mother, Mr. Burden.

YULKA. Oh yes, we have clipped out all the photographs of you and your wife from the society pages.

NINA. Mrs. Burden looks so stylish in all the papers.

JIM. Thank you, Lucie.

NINA. My name's Nina.

JIM. Not Lucie?

LUCIE. No sir, I'm Lucie.

(*The CHILDREN laugh.*)

JIM. Yes, of course, if I stay around very long I'll get you as confused as your mother does. (*THEY all laugh.*) But there are quite a few of you!

ANTONIA. How many have you got, Jim?

JIM. We have no children.

ANTONIA. Oh, ain't that too bad! Maybe you could take one of my bad ones, now? That Leo, he's the worst of all. And I love him the best.

NINA. Mother!

ANTON. It's true, I think she does.

ANTONIA. Ain't it wonderful, Jim, how much people can mean to each other? I'm so glad we had each other when we were little, like mine do.

LUCIE. (*Taking Jim's hand.*) Thank you for coming to see us—I *think* we like you!

JIM. (*Laughing, picking up Lucie.*) I'm sure already that I like you! Now that we've found each other, may, may I come again?

CHILDREN. Yes—please—yes.

JIM. We'll go for picnics up on the Platte river.

LEO. Is it really only five inches deep?

JIM. Let's find out, shall we?

ANTON. Yes, let's do!

JIM. If your folks say it's alright, we'll all have a party on my train out to see Scottsbluff.

(*The CHILDREN are delighted and overwhelmed. THEY reply overlapping each other, almost at the same moment.*)

| LEO. | LUCIE. | ANTON. | NINA. | YULKA. |
|------|--------|--------|-------|--------|
| We're going on a train! | Oh, thank you, Mr. Burden! | None of us have ever been on a train! | I want to go. | Think of it—a train! |

LEO. Please say yes, Mama, please!

ANTONIA. (*Blushing.*) Don't say such things, Jim. We must ask your papa tomorrow.

JIM. It would mean the world to me, Antonia. You see out in those big cities you spoke of, I have found out what a little circle man's experience really is. (*THEY take hands.*) Today with all of you I have at last the sense of coming home to myself.

NINA. Mama, mama. Come see.

(*TONY and ANNIE quickly join ANTONIA. JIMMY and JAMES join JIM. The THREE ANTONIAS and the THREE JIMS join the children on the ground to see Nina's grasshopper.*)

NINA. This big grasshopper seems to be sick. See how he falls over every time he tries to jump?

LUCIE. Is he dead, Mama?

(*The CHILDREN crowd around.*)

ANTONIA. Oh, I hope not. Why don't we help him a little? (*SHE scoops him up with both hands.*) Maybe if we make him warmer he might feel better. (*With great tenderness.*) Shh, shh! Listen children.

*(SHE holds her hands to each child one by one. THEIR
   FACES light up in surprise.)*

ANTONIA. Mu-sic, Mu-sic. Did you see, Jim?
JIM. *(Kneeling with them.)* I remember Antonia, it's a
little Hop Hop!
LEO. A Hop Hop!
AMBROZ. A Hop Hop?

*(All the CHILDREN laugh with the ANTONIAS and
   JIMS. JIM BURDEN takes the "Hop Hop" from
   Antonia's hands and tenderly places it in her hair.)*

JIM. Hop Hop. Mu-sic.

*(EVERYONE echoes this phrase again and again as THEY
   rise and begin to sway, then dance playfully around each
   other. As THEY turn and skip, their turns become more
   exuberant. The ANTONIAS join hands and spin in
   blissful pin wheels, the JIMS mirror their movement.)*

THE 3 ANTONIAS. *(A note of victory.)* MU-SIC!
MU-SIC!

## CURTAIN

## COSTUME PLOT

<u>ANTONIA</u>: petticoat, tights, boots, farm dress, apron
<u>II-2</u>: corset, petticoat, tights, boots, skirt, bodice, overskirt, gloves, hat, jewelry, wig
<u>II-4</u>: **remove** hat, gloves, jewelry
**change into**: nightgown, robe
<u>II-5</u>: same as II-2
<u>II-6</u>: underdress nightgown (used as a blouse), skirt tights boots
<u>II-8</u>: same, add man's hat, overcoat and gloves
<u>II-9</u>: same as I-1

<u>TONY</u>: <u>I-2</u>: corset, petticoat, tights, boots, skirt, blouse, belt, hairpiece
<u>I-7</u>: same
<u>I-11</u>: same
<u>II-1</u>: same, new blouse
<u>II-2</u>: same, add fitted bodice
<u>II-8</u>: same
<u>II-9</u>: same

<u>ANNIE</u>: <u>I-2</u>: slip, tights, boots, dress, pinafore, shawl
<u>I-4</u>: **remove** shawl, pinafore, tights and shoes
<u>I-7</u>: **add** tights, shoes, pinafore
<u>I-8</u>: **add** shawl
<u>I-10</u>: **add** fur hat and mittens
<u>I-11</u>: **add** shawl
<u>II-8</u>: same no shawl, hat or mittens
<u>II-9</u>: same

**JIM BURDEN**: socks, shoes, Norfolk suit, suspenders, shirt, collar, tie, boater, tie pin

I-3: **remove** hat and suit coat

I-11: same **add** suit coat and hat

II-2: same no hat

II-6:.same no hat

II-8: same no hat

II-9: same with hat

**JAMES**: I-2: underwear (short union suit.), socks, shoes, pants, suspenders, shirt with no collar

I-3: same

I-11: same

II-1: same

II-3: same **add** suit coat, collar, tie

II-4: same no collar, tie, suit coat

pg. 99 **remove** pants, shirt and shoes

II-5: same as II-3

II-6: same no collar, suit coat or tie

II-8: same

**JIMMY**: I-1: socks, boots, knickers suit, shirt, hat

I-3: same but **remove** hat and coat during scene and change shirt after bath

I-4: same

I-5: same

I-6: same

I-7: same

I-8: **add** winter coat and hat

I-9: same **remove** coat and **add** sweater

I-10: same

I-11: same **add** coat and hat for funeral

II-6: same no coat, hat or sweater
II-8: same

**JAKE MARPOLE**: I-2: socks, boots, suspenders, trousers, shirt, vest, hat
I-3: socks, boots, suspenders, long underwear shirt, work pants, work shirt, same hat
I-8: **add** barn jacket
I-9:same as I-2-no hat
I-11: same as I-3-**add** coat for funeral
II-5: same as I-2-**add** tie

**MR. SHIMERDA**: I-1: socks, boots, worn but not tattered suit, knitted vest, shirt, neck scarf, coral tie pin, hat, glasses
I-4: same
I-6: same
I-7: same
I-8: same
I-9: same **add** fur collar, hat and knitted mittens

**AMBROZ SHIMERDA**: I-2: socks, boots, suspenders, undershirt, trousers, shirt, short coat, scarf, hat
I-4: same no coat
I-8: same **add** knitted vest
I-11: same **add** hat and knitted mitten for funeral
II-1: socks, boots, suspenders, trousers, shirt, scarf, hat
II-5: same **add** collar, tie and suit coat
II-6: same no coat, tie, collar
II-8: same

**MAREK  SHIMERDA**: <u>I-2</u>: socks, boots, undershirt, trousers, shirt, knitted vest, short coat, knitted hat, webbed gloves (prosthetic), knitted gloves
<u>I-4</u>: same no coat, knitted gloves, hat
<u>I-8</u>: same **add** hat and knitted gloves
<u>I-11</u>: same as I-2

**OTTO FUCHS**: <u>I-2</u>: socks, boots, suspenders, work trousers, work shirt, hat, scarf
<u>I-3</u>: same no hat
<u>I-4</u>: : same **add** hat
<u>I-5</u>: same
<u>I-8</u>: same **add** duster
<u>I-9</u>: same no duster, hat
<u>I-11</u>: same add hat and duster for funeral
<u>II-5</u>: same pants, boots, hat, **add** new shirt, suspenders, vest, scarf

**KRAJIEK**: <u>I-2</u>: socks, boots, trousers, filthy undershirt, filthy overshirt, rope belt, beat-up hat, filthy scarf
<u>I-4</u>: same
<u>I-8</u>: same
<u>I-11</u>: same **add** overcoat

**GRANDFATHER**: <u>I-3</u>: socks, boots, suspenders, work pants, long-sleeved undershirt, work shirt
<u>I-7</u>: same
<u>I-8</u>: same **add** hat and overcoat
<u>I-9</u>: socks, boots, suspenders, suit, shirt, tie
<u>I-11</u>: same **add** hat and overcoat for funeral
<u>II-2</u>: bathrobe, underdress: socks, boots, suit with vest, shirt, tie

II-5: **remove** robe **add** hat
II-7: same no suit coat, hat

**RUSSIAN PETER**: I-5: socks, boots, padding, shirt, trousers, hat
I-7: same

**RUSSIAN PAVEL**: I-5: socks, boots, trousers, shirt, hat
I-7: nightshirt

**MR. CUTTER**: II-1: socks, shoes, suit with vest, shirt with collar, tie
II-4: same no coat, tie
II-5 same as II-1 **add** hat
II-7: same no coat, hat, tie, vest bloodied shirt, and undershirt

**MRS. SHIMERDA**: I-2: tights, boots, petticoat, bodice, skirt, shawl, head scarf
I-4: same, **remove** shawl and bodice, **add** blouse
I-8: same **add** shawl
I-10: same as I-2
I-11: same **add** knitted mittens
II-5: tights, boots, petticoat, **new**: skirt, bodice, shawl, head wrap
II-8: same **remove** shawl and bodice
**add** new blouse

**GRANDMOTHER**: I-3: tights, boots, petticoat, skirt, blouse, apron
I-4: same **add** sunbonnet

I-5: same no sunbonnet
I-8: tights, boot  petticoat, **new**: skirt, bodice, cape, gloves
I-9: same no gloves, cape, **add** apron
I-10: same
I-11: same **add** gloves, and cape for funeral
II-1: tights, **new**: boots, corset, petticoat, bodice, skirt, jewelry
II-2: P. 101 put on robe over clothes
II-5: **add** gloves and hat
II-6: same
II-8: same as I-3

**MRS. HARLING:** II-1: tights, boots petticoat, corset, dickey, bodice, skirt, overskirt, jewelry, wig
II-2: same
II-5: same **add** shoulder cape, hat, gloves.

**FRANCES HARLING:** II-1: tights, boots, petticoat, corset, bodice, skirt, jewelry, wig
II-2: same
II-5: same **add** hat and gloves

**LENA LENGARD:** II-1: tights, pumps, petticoat, corset, bodice, skirt, shoulder cape, hat, gloves, jewelry, hairpiece
II-2: same no cape, hat, gloves
II-3: same **add** hat, gloves, **new**: overskirt
II-5: same as II-1

**TINY SODERBALL**: II-1: striped stockings, pumps, petticoat, corset, bodice, skirt, gloves, hat, jewelry, hairpiece
II-2: same no gloves, hat
II-3: same as II-1: **add** hat, gloves, **new**: overskirt
II-5: as as I-1

**MRS. CUTTER**: II-1: tights, boots, petticoat, corset, dickey, bodice, skirt, hat, wig
II-3: same **add** gloves and shoulder cape
II-5: same

**LEO CUZAK**: I-1: short pants, suspenders, long underwear shirt
II-9: same

**YULKA CUZAK**: I-1: slip, dress, hair band
II-9: same

**NINA CUZAK**: I-1: slip, dress, hair ribbon
II-9: same

**LUCIE CUZAK**: I-1: slip, pinafore, hair bows
II-9: same

**ANTON CUZAK**: I-1: knickers, suspenders, shirt
II-9: same

# CEMENTVILLE
## by Jane Martin
### Comedy
### Little Theatre

(5m., 9f.) Int. The comic sensation of the 1991 Humana Festival at the famed Actors Theatre of Louisville, this wildly funny new play by the mysterious author of *Talking With* and *Vital Signs* is a brilliant portrayal of America's fascination with fantasy entertainment, "the growth industry of the 90's." We are in a run-down locker room in a seedy sports arena in the Armpit of the Universe, "Cementville, Tennessee," with the scurviest bunch of professional wrasslers you ever saw. This is decidedly a small-time operation—not the big time you see on TV. The promoter, Bigman, also appears in the show. He and his brother Eddie are the only men, though; for the main attraction(s) are the "ladies." There's Tiger, who comes with a big drinking problem and a small dog; Dani, who comes with a large chip on her shoulder against Bigman, who owes all the girls several weeks' pay; Lessa, an ex-Olympic shotputter with delusions that she is actually employed presently in athletics; and Netty, an overweight older woman who appears in the ring dressed in baggy pajamas, with her hair in curlers, as the character "Pajama Mama." There is the eager-beaver go-fer Nola, a teenager who dreams of someday entering the glamorous world of pro wrestling herself. And then, there are the Knockout Sisters, refugees from the Big Time but banned from it for heavy-duty abuse of pharmaceuticals as well as having gotten arrested *in flagrante delicto* with the Mayor of Los Angeles. They have just gotten out of the slammer; but their indefatigable manager, Mother Crocker ("Of the Auto-Repair Crockers") hopes to get them reinstated, if she can keep them off the white powder. Bigman has hired the Knockout Sisters as tonight's main attraction, and the fur really flies along with the sparks when the other women find out about the Knockout Sisters. Bigman has really got his hands full tonight. He's gotta get the girls to tear each other up in the ring, not the locker room; he's gotta deal with tough-as-nails Mother Crocker; he's gotta keep an arena full of tanked-up rubes from tearing up the joint—and he's gotta solve the mystery of who bit off his brother Eddie's dick last night.                    (#5580)

**RAVENSCROFT. (Little Theatre.) Mystery.** Don Nigro. 1m., 5f. Simple unit set. This unusual play is several cuts above the genre it explores, a Gothic thriller for groups that don't usually do such things, a thinking person's mystery, a dark comedy that is at times immensely funny and at others quite frightening. On a snowy night, Inspector Ruffing is called to a remote English country house to investigate the headlong plunge of a young manservant, Patrick Roarke, down the main staircase, and finds himself getting increasingly involved in the lives of five alluring and dangerous women— Marcy, the beautiful Viennese governess with a past, Mrs. Ravenscroft, the flirtatious and chattery lady of the manor, Gillian, her charming but possibly demented daughter, Mrs. French, the formidable and passionate cook, and Dolly, a frantic and terrified little maid—who lead him through an increasingly bewildering labyrinth of contradictory versions of what happened to Patrick and to the dead Mr. Ravenscroft before him. There are ghosts at the top of the staircase, skeletons in the closet, and much more than the Inspector had bargained for as his quest to solve one mystery leads him deeper and deeper into others and to an investigation of his own tortured soul and the nature of truth itself. You will not guess the ending, but you will be teased, seduced, bewildered, amused, frightened and led along with the Inspector to a dark encounter with truth, or something even stranger. A funny, first rate psychological mystery, and more.

(#19987)

**DARK SONNETS OF THE LADY, THE. (Advanced Groups.) Drama.** Don Nigro. 4m., 4f. Unit set. First produced professionally at the McCarter Theatre in Princeton and a finalist for the National Play Award, this stunningly theatrical and very funny drama takes place in Vienna in the fall of the year 1900, when Dora, a beautiful and brilliant young girl, walks into the office of Sigmund Freud, then an obscure doctor in his forties, to begin the most famous and controversial encounter in the history of psychoanalysis. Dora is funny, suspicious, sarcastic and elusive, and Freud become fascinated and obsessed by her and by the intricate labyrinth of her illness. He moves like a detective through the mystery of her life, and we meet in the course of his journey through her mind: her lecherous father, her obsessively house-cleaning mother, her irritating brother, her sinister admirer Herr Klippstein and his sensual and seductive wife, and their pretty and lost little governess. Nightmares, fantasies, hallucinations and memories all come alive onstage in a wild kaleidoscopic tapestry as Freud moves closer and closer to the truth about Dora's murky past, and the play becomes a kind of war between the two of them about what the truth is, about the uneasy truce between men and women, and ultimately a tragic love story. Laced throughout with eerie and haunting Strauss waltzes, this is a rich, complex, challenging and delightfully intriguing universe, a series of riddles one inside the other that lead the audience step by step to the center of Dora's troubled soul and her innermost secrets. Is Dora sick, or is the corrupt patriarchal society in which she and Freud are both trapped the real source of a complex group neurosis that binds all the characters together in a dark web of desperate erotic relationships, a kind of beautiful, insane and terrible dance of life, desire and death?

(#5952)

# Other Publications For Your Interest

**PICTURE OF DORIAN GRAY, THE. (Little Theatre.) Drama.** Adapted by John Osborne from the novel by Oscar Wilde. 11m., 4f., plus extras. I Int. w/apron for other scenes. English playwright John Osborne (Look Back in Anger, Inadmissible Evidence, The Entertainer) has given us a brilliant dramatisation of Wilde's classic novel about a young man who, magically, retains his youth and beauty while the decay of advancing years and moral corruption only appears on a portrait painted by one of his lovers. Following the advice of the evil Lord Harry, a cynic who, fashionably, mocks any and all institutions and moral precepts, Dorian comes to believe that the only purpose of life is simply for one to realize, and glorify, one's own nature. In so doing, he is inevitably sucked into the maelstrom of degradation and despair, human nature being what it is. "Osborne has done much more than a scissors-and-paste job on Wilde's famous story. He has thinned out the over-abundant epigrams, he has highlighted the topical concept of youth as a commodity for which one would sell one's soul and he has, in Turn of the Screw fashion, created a sense of evil through implication. Osborne conveys moral disintegration through the gradual breakdown of the hero's language into terse, broken phrases and through a creeping phantasmagoria."—London, The Guardian. "What is so interesting about John Osborne's adaptation of The Picture of Dorian Gray is that he had found in Oscar Wilde's macabre morality a velveted barouche for his own favorite themes. Osborne funks none of the greenery-valley vulgarity of the fabulous story, and conveys much of its fascination."—London, Daily Telegraph. State author when ordering.     **(#18954)**

**FALL OF THE HOUSE OF USHER, THE. (Little Theatre.) Drama.** Gip Hoppe. Music by Jay Hagenbuckle. 6m. 3f. Int. A comfortable suburban family man receives a desperate telephone call from an obscure and forgotten childhood acquaintance. Thus starts a journey into madness that will take Ed Allen to the House of Usher and the terrible secrets and temptations contained there. In this modern adaptation of the classic short story by Edgar Allen Poe, playwright Gip Hoppe takes Gothic horror into the 90s, questioning the definition of "sanity" in the same way Poe did in his day. Ed arrives to find Roderick in a state of panic and anxiety over the impending death of his sister, Madeline. As he tries to sort out the facts, he becomes tangled in a family web of incest and murder. Finding himself infatuated with the beautiful Madeline, his "outside life" fades from his memory as he descends to the depths of madness that inflict all the residents of The House of Usher. *The Fall of the House of Usher* is an exhilarating theatrical adventure leading to an apocalyptic ending that will have audiences thrilled. Actors and designers will be challenged in new ways in this unpredictable and wildly entertaining play. Cassette tape. Use of Mr. Hagenbuckle's music will greatly enhance the play, but it is not mandatory.     **(#7991)**